The Counterfeiters

An Historical Comedy

Wherever there is objective truth there is satire

Wyndham Lewis

THE
Counterfeiters

An Historical Comedy

By Hugh Kenner

WITH DRAWINGS BY GUY DAVENPORT

Indiana University Press   Bloomington & London

for Mary Anne
nutrix formarum mentis

ACKNOWLEDGMENTS

The Counterfeiters was foreseen when drafts of several portions were being written as occasional lectures, but they have since been much expanded and revised. *The Virginia Quarterly Review* published in 1965 a version of chapter II originally delivered at the University of New Mexico as part of a program honoring Marjorie Hope Nicholson, and in 1966 a version of chapter III that was solicited by the English Graduate Students' Club of the University of Virginia. Substantial portions of chapters I and IV are adapted from a lecture delivered at U.C.L.A. as part of the 1963 University of California Faculty Lecture Series, *Humanitas: Retrospect and Prospect*. Chapter IV draws on a lecture written for St. Thomas University, Houston, and later printed in *Spectrum* (Santa Barbara). I have also borrowed passages from two articles written for *National Review*. So the book's indebtedness to editors and sponsoring bodies is heavy; I am grateful for many incentives and generous permissions to reprint and rework. I am also grateful to Mr. Alfred Siegel of New York for suggesting lines of thought and lending materials.

The illustrator has spared no pains to assist the reader's imagination in domains the written word delineates imperfectly.

Contents

Foreword

This book is about the familiar world, three cross-sections of which yield the following:

(1) *Counterfeiting*. Undergraduates used to affront the System by staging a juxtaposition, inventively incongruous: the horse in the bedroom, the Chevy in the lobby, the cow in the bell-tower. But today's fashion is to create a nonexistent student, who by outwitting the System's punch-cards may be carried from Freshman English to Senior Math (Phys Ed being the dangerous salient) and at last installed, in full Bachelorhood, on the Alumni mailing-lists. There is scarcely an academy in the country where this folk art of IBM man has not been attempted.

(2) *Phosphorescent Quotation*. It was long supposed that a politician was best mocked by parody: by isolating traits and exaggerating them. But in the mid-1950's satirists discovered that to mock Dwight Eisenhower it was sufficient to quote him verbatim. Nor was this a function of presidential dyslexia; for in 1961 verbatim excerpts proved John Kennedy's press conferences to be indistinguishable in detail from those of the previous regime. It is now commonplace to remark of a wide range of phenomena that they "parody themselves." Pop art—the contrived application of this principle—was a product of the Kennedy period.

(3) *Connoisseurship*. Antiques were once sought out because they embodied a timeless authority of design sup-

posed to be no longer attainable (Chippendale, Sheraton; and compare the finality of Egyptian sculpture). They are now prized just when no such claims are to be plausibly made for them; only that in some former pocket of time they were purposeful (stained glass lampshades, French telephones; and compare the rectitude of the Cigar Store Indian). This phenomenon is less obscure than its analysts, who circulate the impenetrable term "camp." The artifacts are stylistic quotations; the environment they create is a cultural echo-chamber, reverberant with amusing scraps of dead languages. Things are utterances.

These are generic examples; it is easy to supply many more in each category. We perceive each kind by contrast with an earlier imaginative mode. The first eludes people trained on a poetic of juxtaposition, the second people who understand parody, the third people alert to classic norms. Juxtaposition, parody, the classic norm; the fact that these three obsolete modes summarize, say, the aesthetic of *Ulysses* was part of what Pound meant when he called *Ulysses* an end, not a beginning, or Wyndham Lewis when he called it a terminal moraine. It terminated the Romantic Interlude, which by 16 June 1904 could be said to have become degenerate. Keats's sensuality had declined into Bloom's, Byron's noble savagery into Boylan's, Shelley's élan into Stephen's. In the music, the painting, the theatre and the literature of that time corresponding postures had evolved, all ridiculous, all seen by normal people as normal. Joyce's strategy was to reduce them by juxtaposition, by parody, by the evocation of classic norms. He terminated an era. He also pointed forward to another, counterfeiting a document, quoting actual sources, cutting the reader free among unweighted facts earmarked by many times.

Nearly fifty years after *Ulysses,* juxtaposition has wholly given way to counterfeiting, in a world of image-duplicators; parody to quotation, in a world of nonfictional fiction; classicizing to eclectic connoisseurship, in a world that has turned into one huge *musée sans murs.*

By counterfeit, by quotation, by connoisseurship: the great artists of an astonishing half-century, 1690-1740, proceeded so. We call them satirists, they called themselves (having no better word) satirists; they were, Swift and Pope, great realists, great modernists. They had responded, we are going to see, to a new definition of man, proper to the new universe of empirical fact, which definition still obtains because we are still in that universe. They transmuted, to the point of destruction, the old ritual genres, tragedy, comedy, epic, which were proper to an older universe. They were at the leading edge of an age which was moving toward an age like our own, at home with the machine and with utter ambivalence. The mind of Europe, unable to face machine or ambivalence, retreated (after an ominous calm) into the Romantic Interlude, restoring the genres since phenomena were held to be inherently sad, funny, noble, making a value of the pure intention, and achieving meanwhile such memorable feats (its adrenalin roused like a frightened stag's) as quite to conceal its posture of retreat. This movement ran down into nonsense, having pretended for one hundred fifty years that a world created by human beings was not human. And it was finally cauterized (1910-1930) by juxtaposition, parody, classic norms; and now we pick up the old themes, the themes miscalled Neoclassical, the themes best summarized (in a Xerox age) by invoking the aesthetic of the counterfeiter, that patient historical novelist.

Not that we now shut off the Romantic discoveries: they are part of our ineluctable past. But a Robert Creeley's spontaneities are knowing in our way, not Coleridgean, despite Creeley's affection for Coleridge's stanza. I hope to persuade the reader of what follows that to call them counterfeit is to praise them relevantly.

This exposition will include, because its subject did, a variety of themes which the Dewey Decimal system (a Romantic artifact) prefers to keep in different parts of the building: the Enlightenment; Buster Keaton (stoic comedian); bad poetry; Albrecht Dürer; Joyce; Swift, Pope; closed systems, mathematical and mechanical; Charles Babbage and his Calculating Engines; the late history of Latin abstract nouns; Andy Warhol; Gödel's Proof; horses, computers, games; a clockwork duck that suffered from indigestion; and a man who wore a gas mask to ride his bicycle. It examines from a somewhat different angle a sampling of the phenomena looked at in my earlier book *The Stoic Comedians* (1963); if the two angles yield a stereoscopic view, they also embrace largely different fields, with less overlap than supplementation. The reader who wants to reconcile the two books should consider their two governing eyes as located on opposite planes of the same head, like a Houyhnhnm's. The terrain remains continuous, and some is common to both.

So much for orienting landmarks. Now goodbye earth. Henceforward the exposition will hover freely. It starts with Satire.

The Counterfeiters

An Historical Comedy

I

Counterfeitable Man

The satirist presses to some provisional conclusion a way of defining man, a way we had thought and contrive to still think plausible, though as long as we still so think the satire will irk us. Roman man is urban man, endowed man, man responsive to the resources of civilization: this is man, he is the enabled animal. Yes, says Juvenal. Enlightened man is sensitive to allay suffering and scrupulous to remove dirt. He makes no pother, things are to be done economically, sensibly. This is man, he is the sensible animal. Yes, says a pamphleteer, and here is my Modest Proposal. Methodical man takes note, and takes stock, and lets no fact escape remark and no premise fail of its consequence. He is attentive to natural forces, indeed to the useful travails of dumb beasts, and knows his place above them, being gifted with speech and reason. This is man, he is the rational animal. Indeed, says a retired seaman from Nottinghamshire, and what is more I could take you to some fine talking horses.

They call themselves Houyhnhnms. They look like horses and they talk like Bertrand Russell. They have no judiciary, and what a lawyer does must be explained to them, along with the nature of "begging, robbing, stealing, cheating, pimping, forswearing, flattering, suborning, forging, gaming, lying, fawning, hectoring, voting, scribbling, star-gazing, poisoning, whoring, canting, libelling, free-thinking, and the like occupations: every one of which terms, I was at much pains to make [them] understand." Are they perhaps better men than man?

Or consider this candidate for manhood. It looks like a switchboard and it computes like an angel. In mere microseconds it can ascertain the nth term of a Fourier Series and multiply by the number it first thought of. Does it think as we do? Better? What does it feel like, to scintillate like that? Does it feel? May it have a soul? To say no, thought one great logician, is to presume against the omnipotence of the Almighty, who has surely "freedom to confer a soul on an elephant if He sees fit," and if He does not see fit is doubtless guided by the insufficiency of an elephant's reasoning power. But "in attempting to construct such machines we should not be irreverently usurping His power of creating souls, any more than we are in the procreation of children; rather we are, in either case, instruments of His will providing mansions for the souls that He creates."[1]

This logician (Alan M. Turing, the Spinoza of computers) becomes by our criterion a considerable satirist. He presses to a provisional conclusion the idea that there may well be a soul, or as good as, where there is a sufficiency of reason; and as to whether humanoid form connotes a sufficiency of reason, he alludes to "the polite con-

1. Alan M. Turing, "Thought and Machine Intelligence," *Mind*, October 1950; reprinted in J. R. Newman, *The World of Mathematics*, N. Y., 1956, vol. IV, 2099-2123.

vention that everyone thinks." We shall be meeting Turing again, when he is mounted on a defective bicycle, as though to enact man's relation to the mechanism with which he is lucklessly entoiled. We shall learn that Turing carried to its definitive formulation the theme of the Counterfeit Man. But later, later.

Meanwhile we may be profitably asking, has Robinson Crusoe a soul? He has many thoughts, and much practical reason. He enjoys a cultural heritage (the tool chest), and the wit to make use of it (a lobster would not have, nor a Congolese, nor even a digital computer). He grows, moreover, in piety, ever day by day adequating his sentiments to those sanctioned by his Creator. And he has written a book, as not even the wisest Houyhnhnm has done. He has surely a soul? But the best divines say no. They say he does not exist. They call the book counterfeit.

There is (A. D. 1966) a mathematician named Bourbaki,[2] attested to by numerous papers in the mathematical journals. He too does not exist. He too has (therefore?) no soul. He is the pseudonym of a self-renewing syndicate, its average age always optimal, which meets annually on the French Riviera to plot strategy.

And the soul of Betty Crocker? There is no soul of Betty Crocker, though women of the same name have doubtless souls.

The Collège de 'Pataphysique evaluated in 1956 the man of letters Jean Paulhan (who had doubted whether a certain Dr. Sandomir existed) by circulating neat cards[3] on which was engraved

2. John Kobler, "Who is Bourbaki?," *Saturday Evening Post*, Feb. 26, 1966, 34-35.
3. Evergreen Review, #13, 154.

> # *Jean Paulhan*
> ## *n'existe pas*

Jean Paulhan has (1966) nevertheless a soul. He edits the *Nouvelle Revue Française,* if that is evidence. He wrote (1962) the "Préface" to *Histoire d'O,* by Pauline Réage, concerning whom the consensus is that she does not exist, though somebody (Jean Paulhan? surely not?) presumably wrote her book.

And in 1964 the writer of these present pages (who here affirms his existence) signed his name, in Paris, in a visitors' book below the signatures of Jean Paulhan and Jorge Luis Borges. And Borges, some years earlier, had considered that he was attended by an *alter ego* named Borges, one of the pair having a soul, and one (not the same?) having written an account of how certain volumes of the *Encyclopaedia Britannica* were counterfeited so as to circulate allusions to a realm called Tlön, with "transparent tigers and towers of blood:" which realm (let us affirm, in vertigo) "does not exist."[4]

We are deep, these days, in the counterfeit, and have long since had to forego easy criteria for what is "real." (And a counterfeit banknote is real.) We have sunk so deep into dubiety that our finest satire is discoverable in technical publications, where writers simply describe how things are exactly. (And the most harrowing book of our principal comic writer is entitled *How It Is;* almost his next deed was Buster Keaton's last film script.) Thus in the Pro-

4. Jorge Luis Borges, *Labyrinths*, N. Y., 1962. See the stories "Borges and I" and "Tlön, Uqbar, Orbis Tertius."

ceedings of the Third London Symposium on Information Theory (1956) we find clerical activities, on which the West expends perhaps a third of its mind, summed up as "moving things about according to the marks on them," a task performed by "appropriately coupled devices for observing and manipulating—that is, 'clerks'." We learn that "power consumption increases with the cube of the speed at which clerical operations are carried out," and that "a typewriter is itself a clerical system in which marked and markable objects are manipulated according to rule." Clerks, moreover, "have finite resolving power,"[5] a quasi-pun gratifying to whoever has observed an assistant teller in a state of irresolution. Gulliver in just this way explains to his Houyhnhnm master what lawyers are, what warriors are, what judges are, what doctors are. The Lilliputian commission in just this way describes what it found in the pockets of the Man Mountain (his watch, which makes "an incessant Noise like that of a Water-Mill," is presumably "the God that he worships," since he never does anything without consulting it). The wise men of Brobdingnag in just this way describe Gulliver: not indeed as an appropriately coupled device for observing and manipulating, for they never observe him doing anything clerical, but as a carnivorous animal adapted neither for running, nor climbing trees, nor digging holes in the earth. These are all attempts to define a thing—a clerk, a watch, a man—by function or observed fitness for function, whether because we do not know, in the usual way, "what it is," or prefer to deem such knowl-

5. R. A. Fairthorne, "Some Clerical Operations and Languages," in *Information Theory: Third London Symposium*, ed. Colin Cherry, N. Y. and London, 1956, 111-120.

edge irrelevant, or have methodically interfered with our usual means of observing it, so that it no longer looks like what it is.

The wise men of Brobdingnag were conceived by a wise man of Dublin, who had observed how the telescope or the microscope could impair the human faculties, turning for instance an ivory miniature into delinquent smears of pigment.[6] Are such instruments the playthings of folly, or is the face in the portrait a function merely of our deficient senses, concerning which we do well to undeceive ourselves? Is a handsome woman merely imperfectly seen? To the eye of Gulliver a Maid of Honor's giant torso, quite as through Galileo's optic glass the round moon, disintegrates into coarse detail: the skin uneven, "with a Mole here and there as broad as a Trencher, and Hairs hanging from it thicker than Pack-threads."[7] And disregarding blemishes on that skin, is any familiar amenity more than a skin of appearance? "Last Week I saw a Woman *flay'd*," writes one of Swift's busy personae, "and you will hardly believe, how much it altered her Person for the worse."[8] Appearance, appearance: and the world is perhaps a congeries of appearances, imperfectly observed? (David Hume was to think so.) Observe one appearance with care, and record the observation: you have a Fact. A dog with eighteen ounces of water pumped into its thorax grew short-winded. Record another: a dog injected with opium, brandy and water, died. Another: a die swallowed by a dog was excreted after twenty-four hours, its weight halved

6. Irvin Ehrenpreis, *Swift: The Man, his Works, and the Age*, Cambridge (Mass.), 1962, 83.
7. *Gulliver's Travels*, II-v.
8. *A Tale of a Tub*, ix.

but its shape and spots retained. All these things were noted at the Dublin Philosophical Society in the 1680's, when Swift was an undergraduate.[9] Do they help us know what a dog is? A dog is perhaps partially defined as that animal which is inconvenienced in one way by water in the thorax, but in another way by brandy in the jugular, and has the power of halving the bulk of dice. Or granted that these conditions (which no one earlier would have thought to observe) are insufficient to specify dogginess, what conditions are? Is there such a thing as dogness, as a dog, or do we merely triangulate shifting points? Dogness, horseness, manness: *caninitas, equinitas, humanitas:* such terms, denoting stable essences, men in the seventeenth century were learning increasingly to view with suspicion, as being part of the empty terminology of the schools.

"Ancients" could join with "moderns" in reprobating such uses of the long words ending in *-tas,* since they do not correspond to classical ways of thinking. They became technical terms in that tract of time the enlightened had learned to call Gothic, and many of them do not occur in classical writers at all. The famous *Equinitas,* horseness, whose implications Swift was to find so suggestive, seems to have been coined by the late twelfth century Latin translators of Avicenna and put into circulation by Duns Scotus, the Augustans' archetypal Dunce.

These new words, when they were new, denoted a new kind of meaning, presenting for isolated inspection the essence which makes the thing that thing which it is. The classical abstract nouns on which they were patterned—*humilitas, facilitas, gravitas*—simply gave substantial

9. Ehrenpreis, 83. The whole of Part I, ch. 8, is relevant.

form to some adjective, and denoted qualities felt as essentially adjectival: of being humble, of being easy, of being heavy. Such qualities may come and go, may be present in greater or lesser degree, or not at all. But *Equinitas* is either there or it is not. Like the other nouns of the schoolmen it has no adjectival residue. Such nouns denote (as nouns should) stable and substantial objects of investigation: that quality (*Equinitas*) of being horse, by the possession of which all horses, and no other beings, are distinguished from all other things that walk, or move, or die.

And so with the schoolmen's *Humanitas*. No man can not have it, no man has it more than another man. But does it exist? The mind of Swift's age was beginning to think not. When analysis has not yet disclosed how a watch knows what time it is, the watch is mysterious; and men were perhaps only mysterious in that way. Observe their behavior, according to the best empiric disciplines, as you observe a watch's behavior; and when you have observed thoroughly you will know all there is to know about man. Observe their courtship rituals, for example:

> If we inspect into the usual Process of modern Courtship, we shall find it to consist in a devout Turn of the Eyes, called *Ogling;* an artificial Form of Canting and Whining by rote, every Interval, for want of other Matter, made up with a Shrug, or a Hum, a Sigh or a Groan; The Style compact of insignificant Words, Incoherences and Repetition. These, I take to be the most accomplish'd Rules of Address to a Mistress; and where are these performed with more Dexterity, than by the *Saints*?[10]

This is Swift working out a comparison between religious

10. Swift, *Mechanical Operation of the Spirit*, ii.

and amatory enthusiasts. It is also a set of instructions for programming a Courting Machine, which a few trifling adjustments will convert into a Canting Machine; it will be impossible to distinguish such a machine from a man courting or canting, especially as there will be no need to simulate intelligible speech, and thus to confront the problem whether the machine understands what it is saying. Swift is quite explicit about this:

> . . . in the Language of the Spirit, *Cant* and *Droning* supply the place of *Sense* and *Reason*, in the Language of Men: Because, in Spiritual Harangues, the Disposition of Words according to the Art of Grammar, hath not the least Use, but the Skill and Influence wholly lye in the Choice and Cadence of the Syllables. . . .

A human specialization, sufficiently well observed, is mechanically reproducible, and when a man has *become* his specialization, that man (Swift's Puritan, or Lover) is himself mechanically reproducible; and the tract from which we have been quoting is *A Discourse Concerning the Mechanical Operation of the Spirit*.

The Mechanical Operation of the Body is easier to simulate, suggested as it is by the cyclical pattern of so many bodily activities, from the circulation of the blood (announced by Harvey in 1628) to the reduplicated stride of walking legs. The King of Brobdingnag, when he saw Gulliver walking, at first supposed that he might be "a piece of clock-work (which is in that country arrived to a very great perfection) contrived by some ingenious artist," and was only undeceived when he heard the mannikin speak Brobdingnagian. Speech, until the twentieth century, was a prime difficulty for the counterfeiter; Descartes himself, the arch-mechanist, for whom the human body may "be considered as a kind of machine, so made up and composed of bones, nerves, muscles, veins, blood and skin, that although there were in it no mind, it would still exhibit the same motions which it at present manifests,"[11] yet supposed that such a machine, constructed by an artisan, would give itself away when someone tried to converse with it, "for we may easily conceive a machine to be so constructed that it emits vocables . . . but not that it should arrange them variously so as appositely to reply to what is said in its presence, as men of the lowest grade of intellect can do."[12]

Swift was less sure. He made collections of Genteel Conversation, of which the purport was that prefabricated silliness was exchanged, all over England, by talking dolls. He also, as everyone knows, made horses talk, and teach a man their language, and was at pains to insist that the horses' language, as well as their sentiments, emanated from the unimpeded intercourse between rational beings and an orderly world. Thus either speech is sheer behavior, and a parrot can simulate it, or it is sheer concatenated reason, and a fine machine can simulate it: perhaps a fine machine shaped like a horse, and composed of bones, nerves, muscles, veins, blood and skin.

Satire stems from such clear definitions. So also does mechanism; for Swift's age was groping toward a principle familiar to ours, that you can be said to understand a process thoroughly if you know how to instruct a machine

11. Descartes, *Meditations on the First Philosophy*, vi.
12. Descartes, *Discourse on Method*, v.

Empirical Study of Art of Sinking,
Third Decade, Twentieth Century

to carry it out. ("To understand is to construct," said da Vinci.) This makes a related proposition seem plausible: to the extent that you can simulate an organism, to that extent you understand what it is.

For to return to our laboratory dog, bloated by water, killed by brandy, challenged by swallowed dice: we can easily devise a mechanism which water will slow, and brandy halt, and through which dice will pass at the cost of half their volume; and if these are the necessary and sufficient specifications for a dog, we who have abandoned faith in a hovering *caninitas* must agree that that machine will be a dog. Let no one object that they are outrageous specifications: experiment has shown that common dogs meet them, so they must be met. True, although necessary they are not sufficient. Experience calls also for a bark: well, we can add one; and for a wagging tail: nothing simpler. It is easy to think of more and more and more criteria, but not to think of any the mechanician could not simulate; and by 1738 Jacques de Vaucanson (1709-1782) had exhibited in Paris a mechanical duck which could waddle and splash, beat the air with detailed feathered wings, wag its head, quack, pick up grain, ingest this with swallowing movements, and eventually excrete the residue: for the production of which latter "it was necessary in a little space to construct a chemical laboratory, to decompose the main constituents [of the grain] and cause them to issue forth at will." Each wing contained four hundred moving pieces. Had Andersen heard of this miraculous fowl when he conceived the Emperor's Nightingale, the same that Yeats set in Byzantium, "miracle, bird or golden handiwork," divining in its "glory of changeless metal" a mortal poet's apotheosis? This gadget meets so many of the specifications for duckness (*anatitas*? duck is *anas*) that we can easily imagine any others we like being met; and sure enough, by 1847 a Swiss named Rechsteiner had constructed an improved version which suffered from indigestion, and simulated abdominal contractions followed by a malodorous evacuation. "The truth is," reported a contemporary, "that the smell which now spreads through the room becomes almost unbearable. We wish to express to the artist-inventor the pleasure which his demonstration gave to us."[13] Clearly the limiting case will be a counterfeit duck so perfect that it will fail to meet one criterion only, that of not having been manufactured, but hatched from an egg.

What is being forged, we may say, what we are at bottom being asked to believe in, is not the duck but the duck's hatching; sufficient trouble over waddle, quack, excrement and feathers will persuade us of the unproducible natal egg. This is an important general law: the counterfeiter's real purpose is to efface himself, like the Flaubertian artist, so that we will draw the conclusion he wants us to draw about how his artifact came into existence. Thus it is difficult to discover any objection to a forged Vermeer, except that Vermeer did not paint it; to a forged banknote, except that the bank did not issue it; to the *Journal of the Plague Year*, except that it is not the journal it purports to be, but a fabrication; or to Crusoe's narrative, except that there was no Crusoe. Nor is it easy to decide whether

13. A. Chapuis and E. Droz, *Automata*, Neuchâtel, 1958, 233-242; S. Giedion, *Mechanization Takes Command*, N. Y., 1948, 35. Chapuis and Droz display four pathetic photographs of what remains of the Vaucanson mechanism.

a man who has made a banknote is a government employee, a counterfeiter, or a pop artist, unless we have evidence of how he meant his work to be regarded. A prestigious case was made in the 1940's for a criticism that should look only at the artifact, never at evidence of the artificer's intention;[14] but it is difficult to grant a more than provisional usefulness to the theory of the Intentional Fallacy when it covertly glances at a modern title-page to ascertain who did write *Robinson Crusoe*, all the time protesting that it considers the object alone. For our knowledge that *Robinson Crusoe* is fiction, not memoir, alters *Robinson Crusoe* profoundly, as the fiction of Jorge Luis Borges clearly shows.[15]

Crusoe exemplifies the age's most frontal attack on the problem of counterfeiting speech; reduce the speech to writing, reduce the writing to print, and the task is enormously simplified. One loose end remains, a chirography someone may demand to inspect. Swift dealt with that by causing Gulliver's cousin Sympson to permit the handwritten ms of the *Travels* to be destroyed, a negligence concerning which Gulliver is understandably testy.[16] The script from which the printer worked, moreover, was mysteriously dropped, by arrangement with Mr. A. Pope, at the publisher's house "in the dark, from a hackney coach," after Swift had left England.[17] These somewhat cum-

14. "The Intentional Fallacy," by W. K. Wimsatt Jr. and Monroe C. Beardsley, reprinted in Prof. Wimsatt's *The Verbal Icon,* Lexington, Ky., 1954.

15. "Pierre Menard, Author of the Quixote," in *Labyrinths* (the reader unfamiliar with this story will find it summarized on pages 90-91, following).

16. "A Letter, from Capt. Gulliver, to his Cousin Sympson," added by Swift to the 1735 edition.

17. Bonamy Dobrée, *Alexander Pope,* London, 1963, 60.

bersome arrangements, which reflect in perhaps equal parts fear of the censor and delighted pursuit of logic, were not improved on until Bram Stoker arranged that the sole authority for *Dracula,* following the destruction (within the work) of diaries, letters and dictaphone cylinders alike, should be a pile of perfectly inscrutable typescript. (The machine is always the counterfeiter's ally.)

And alas, the Augustans immediately realized, who can trust a merely printed—or even a once recopied—document? Hence the busy speculation concerning who, precisely, had written what; and the trouble to which Pope and Swift were not seldom put, to disavow their own work ("I doubt whether the *Tale of a Tub* be his," said Dr. Johnson in 1763, "for he never owned it, and it is much above his usual manner."[18]) Hence, to the undying consternation of the eighteenth century "Ancients," the scandal created by the great Richard Bentley (1662-1742), who just at the turn of the century showed the Letters of Phalaris (sixth century B.C.) to be forgeries dating some thousand years after Phalaris died, if indeed he ever existed.

For grant the principle on which counterfeiting rests, that a man is knowable only in his behavior, and, when he is dead or otherwise out of sight, only in the traces his behavior has left; grant that, and the authority of the Ancients, doughty men whom we had been accustomed to treating (Tully, Maro) with the familiarity we accord living eminences, dwindles to a problem in the evidential consistency of scraps of paper.

Sir William Temple had asserted on behalf of pristine wisdom, that "the two most ancient authors that I know

18. Boswell, *Life of Johnson,* July 28, 1763.

of in prose . . . are Aesop's Fables and Phalaris's Epistles, both living near the same time, which was that of Cyrus and Pythagoras. As the first has been agreed by all ages since for the greatest master of his kind, . . . so I think the Epistles of Phalaris to have more race, more spirit, more force of wit and genius, than any others I have ever seen, either ancient or modern." Temple's was a familiar theme, whether or not his examples were. Our civilization is nourished by a strong vein of wisdom running from remote antiquity. And the comfort of contemplating this *vis perennis* Bentley destroyed, by asserting that nothing of Aesop's was extant and that Phalaris' letters were a manifest hoax: for he mentions towns which were not built, and quotes books which had not been written, and uses a dialect unknown until five centuries after he died. Being flayed, Phalaris' person is altered greatly for the worse We are left the book, to be sure, but its author is transformed into an Alexandrian sophist, and not an honest one either: an embarrassing application of the principle that the counterfeiter creates not a text but an author. The text he merely confects. In an age which looked to antiquity not for books but for men, Bentley was asking inconvenient questions. Homer himself was to dissolve into a committee before Bentley's century was out; indeed Bentley by 1713 had already reduced "Homer" to the composer of "a sequel of songs and rhapsodies, to be sung by himself for small earnings and good cheer";[19] in 1732 he was even to attack "Milton" frontally, and disintegrate him into (1) a blind poet, (2) an ill-lettered amanuensis, and (3) an officious interpolator who wrote all the illogical

19. R. C. Jebb, *Bentley*, London, 1909, 146.

bits: as when a swarming multitude is said to issue from the barbarous North's "frozen loins."[20] Either these three in unwitting concert invented "Milton," or, as we tend to think, Bentley invented them; it is wonderful what a swarming of ghostly persons textual studies cannot help but imply, for a blunder, no less than an imposture, requires that we postulate the man who committed it, or else concede that Homer did little but nod.

But these multiplied fallible men, bards, scribes, editors, recensionists, outright fakers, are not those sturdy foursquare Ancients whose wisdom first shook and then sustained the world. They buzz in the vicinity of mere texts, which now occupy, like a duck's characteristics, the foreground, and behind which *auctoritas,* like *anatitas,* dissolves. Hence (Alexander Pope foresaw) a long twilight, a vertigo of classicism into fuddyduddy chaos and lexicographic catatonia. Hence Pope's assault, misattributed to the jealousy which merely pointed it, on Bentley the "awful Aristarch," who dim'd the eyes and stuff'd the head "With all such reading as was never read," and roundly proclaimed,

> In ancient Sense if any needs will deal,
> Be sure I give them Fragments, not a Meal; . . .
> The critic Eye, that microscope of Wit,
> Sees hairs and pores, examines bit by bit:
> How parts relate to parts, or they to whole,
> The body's harmony, the beaming Soul,
> Are things which Kuster, Burman, Wasse shall see,
> When Man's whole frame is obvious to a *Flea.*

When this was written Gulliver's account of the pocky breasts of court ladies had been in the poet's memory some

20. Jebb, 185.

sixteen years, so it is not surprising to find Bentley's mind, before which Beauty exploded into minute inappropriatenesses, compared to a microscope.

Robinson Crusoe contains a famous error: Crusoe is made to swim naked to the wreck and then fill his pockets with spoils. This is the sort of thing Bentley would have emended in an ancient text, as he altered the reference of Horace (*Ep.* I. vii. 29) to a fox eating grain. He expected logic, he expected "correctness," the criteria of the impenetrable counterfeit. Logic and correctness cohere about a pseudo-person (an automaton is *perfectly* logical), which Bentley tended to expect where there were merely real people, such as Q. Horatius Flaccus and John Milton. He may stand as synecdoche for the scholars, intuited with such accurate panic by the Augustan wits, who removed from behind the classical texts the persons whose moral authority had drawn men's minds to those texts for more than a thousand years: the classics were consistently read as moral authorities, and authority stems from a person. Those persons gone—Phalaris (for what he is worth) evaporated, Aesop eponymized, Homer disintegrated, Horace rendered fallible—two new justifications for classical study were eventually devised: the discipline of having paradigms beaten into one, and the gratifications of "aesthetics." Virgil was no longer wise, but ah, he was beautiful: balanced: stuffed with patterned vowels and recurrences.

Yet amid balance and echo man lusts for authority: for a personal voice. "The letter killeth, the spirit giveth life." "The spirit killeth, the letter giveth life." These two texts are equally grave, equally poised, aesthetically gratifying alike. St. Paul wrote one and T. S. Eliot the other. Though contradictory, they are even equally plausible. Yet it seems to matter, which is which: which the saint, which the poet. Similarly, when Shakespeare replaced the very shaky classics as the moral oracle of Anglo-Saxonry, Shakespeare the lecherous actor had in turn to be replaced by some weightier person, to underwrite those insights; and high-mindedness was soothed by a newly-invented Francis Bacon, playwright, whose principal invention in turn was a playwright named William Shakespeare.

As fire drives out fire, so the remedy for the ills that stem from our consciousness of pervasive counterfeiting is to counterfeit. So we devise ideal men, called the norms of Tests, for people to be cowed by; and then we devise procedures to help people pass Tests.

So the eighteenth century, having arrived at Counterfeitable Man, absolved itself not by reprobating the concept but by multiplying counterfeit men: Crusoe and Gulliver, sober narrators; Ossian, an epic poet like "Homer," preferred by Napoleon; and (seeing that Satire stems from definitions) its mode of high art was Satire; and (seeing that definitions lead to automata) it made of its defined men working models: of man defined as executioner (the guillotine), and of man defined as chessplayer (von Kempelen's automaton, which was not only a counterfeit man but a counterfeit counterfeit, since it concealed a man), and of man defined as compassionate reformer of Ireland (the "author" of the Modest Proposal). These models are all incipient or overt ventures in satire: for imagine, just as we imagine Swift's grim proposer, a kindly middle-aged man who proposes, in implementation of the equality of man, every man's right to be executed in the same way as the nobility, by beheading; and moreover by a functionary whose skill and speed no bribe would intensify; imagine him then describing the automaton he has designed to ensure all this, to the unspeakable augment of equality and fraternity. Swift himself has no more devious a logic to disorient us with; but no Swift invented Dr. Joseph-Ignace Guillotin, who presented his case before the National Assembly of France, December 1, 1789.

In a happier France, Vaucanson who made the duck made a flute-player, his leather-tipped fingers moving over stops that obstructed an air-pump.[21] Like the guillotine, this is rigidly specialized; the task of programming it for a different tune was almost beyond a later craftsman's powers. Later craftsmen all over Europe maintained the tradition, and Vaucanson's inspiration eventually descended to the man who made a twelve-inch Silver Lady, "an admirable *danseuse,* with a bird on the fore finger of her right hand, which wagged its tail, flapped its wings, and opened its beak. This lady attitudinized in a most fascinating manner. Her eyes were full of imagination, and irresistible."[22] So a little boy remembered her, having been taken by his mother to a house in Hanover Square, London, where a man called Merlin presided over an exhibit of mechanical wonders. It was the very end of the eighteenth century.

That boy inherited sufficient means to buy, years later, the ruined Silver Lady from Merlin's successors; he pos-

---

21. Chapuis and Droz, 273-277.
22. Charles Babbage, *Passages from the Life of a Philosopher,* London, 1864, 17.

sessed such intelligence, and by manhood had so far developed his mechanical aptitude, that he was able to restore her workings, for exhibition to company in his drawing-room;[23] and his mathematical bent, which won him at thirty-six Newton's chair, the Lucasian Professorship at Cambridge, was so far married to Vaucanson's tradition of clockwork simulation that he had ready in his rooms a mechanism of his own devising to keep the Lady company: an Engine for computing tables by the method of constant differences. It would clack away cheerfully, once programmed and set in motion, and signal any encounters with imaginary roots by ringing bells.[24] He was Charles Babbage, the father of the computer; and the Analytical Engine, a wholly general digital computer on which he expended in vain the latter half of a long life, was to have taken instructions from punched cards by a principle Babbage borrowed about 1834 from the Jacquard loom, which Jacquard in turn had developed thirty years earlier while restoring in the Paris Conservatoire des Arts et Métiers a loom devised (after principles taken from the clockwork flautist) by Vaucanson.[25] So by two direct lines of succession, via automata and via weaving machinery, the maker of ducks and fluteplayers to the Ancien Régime inspired the great British prophet of cerebral mechanization, intuiter of the giant winking Brains before which we cower.

Babbage will occupy us further: we shall be sampling his informed enthusiasm (from which no one would guess

23. Babbage, *Passages*, 365.
24. Babbage, *Passages*, 66.
25. Giedion, *Mechanization Takes Command*, 36.

that mills are dark and satanic) for the rationale of the Victorian factory, a wholly mechanized environment. Here Vaucanson was again the forerunner: having been named Inspector of the Silk Manufactures he planned and built near Lyons about 1756 the first wholly rationalized industrial plant in the world, linked machines executing all processes from the cocoons onward, the whole driven by a single overshot waterwheel. Temperature and moisture were regulated, but for the benefit of the silk, not the workers;[26] these latter were the first men in the world to know they were spending their waking hours wholly inside a single vast coordinated machine, whose dependencies they were.

The visible is preceded by the ideal. Already numerous Englishmen had elected to deliver their consciousness to a circumambient machine, but one that could not be seen: a mechanical universe (Newton's) which permeated the mind with the aid of an automated language (the Royal Society's dearest, most comprehensive project). That is what the new clarity of English after 1670 comes to: a language which, to the degree that you master its usages and trim your thought to its regnant norms of elegance, compels you to behave as if you were a rational animal, giving your mind to prescribed linkages between thing and thing. (The Romantics were to find the ensuing strain too great to be borne.) Bishop John Wilkins, commissioned by the Royal Society to tidy up human discourse, went so far as to reduce to tables "all simple things and notions, by a Consideration of them *à Priori,*" and then attempted the reduction of "all other Words in the Dictionary

26. Giedion, 36.

to these Tables, either as they were *Synonymous* to them, or to be *defined* by them," and then went on to "such a *Natural Grammar,* as might be suited to the Philosophy of Speech."[27]

Such interests thinned and sharpened English diction, and made the norm of style a tidy logic. Whoever subscribes to its discipline is Counterfeitable Man par excellence. Since his thought runs from considerations *a priori,* any phase of it can be imitated, even mechanized, as Babbage's clockwork mathematician was to demonstrate. The computer simulates thought when thought has been defined in a computer's way; the automaton simulates man when man has been defined in an automaton's way.

There were automata long before Vaucanson—histories of the subject commence with Hero of Alexandria (first century A.D.). There were mechanical aids to computation before Babbage—Pascal designed a digital adding machine. But Hero and Pascal would not have called their artifacts simulators, but rather toys or tools, utilized by men who were metaphysically something other. The eighteenth and nineteenth centuries were less sure that man was other. To trace, in their automata, an advanced technology derived from looms and watches, enlightens us less than does consideration of their novel uncertainties about where, if indeed it existed, the boundary between man and simulacrum lay. If a man does nothing with his life but spin threads, then just how is a thread-spinning machine not a purified man? And indeed it can replace him.

27. John Wilkins, D.D., Dean of Ripon, and Fellow of the Royal Society, *An Essay Towards a Real Character and a Philosophical Language*, London, 1668. Quotations from the unpaginated "Epistle to the Reader."

Such questions are not rhetorical. Impressed by the philosophical ideas of his day, the young Vaucanson first came up to the capital intending nothing less than to synthesize real life.[28] The duck and the flute-player were partial fulfilments of this ambition; it would have been difficult, in the terminology of the Encyclopaedists, to maintain that they were not merely curtailed by a defective technology, but metaphysically insufficient.

Not the automaton, but the concept of counterfeitable man, was the age's characterizing achievement. On such a man—man only empirically known—rationality is impressed from all directions, from his language, from his work, from his machines. He is installed not amidst a Creation but in a system: in many systems, simultaneous systems. Systems expect that we will comply with them; and in a society which forces man to behave like a rational animal, completing 1040A and coping with schedules, human behavior, human artifacts, will be by definition phases of satire. And (witness the familiar notion that this or that "parodies itself") the relevant art will be what we now call "pop": will be copies of those artifacts. Emma Bovary, for whom fiction offers not dreams but achievable patterns—a norm of feminine behavior and a compendium of life's rich promises—Emma is the programmed woman, and *Madame Bovary* (1857), knowingly simulating the popular novelist's gestures, is to those novels what the work of a Roy Lichtenstein is to our comic books.

Systems expect that we will comply with them. In rapid proliferation, for a dozen decades, systems were elaborated, and the corresponding men excogitated: economic

28. Chapuis and Droz, 233.

man, natural man, political man, scientific man, all of them men who inhabit each one his appropriate universe, a universe where there are none but economic forces, or none but natural, or none but political. Any such man, inserted into mankind's actual universe, would have certain disorientations to cope with, the coordinates according to which he was defined being absent, or blurred, or intercrossed with others. Defined man is an anomaly; defined man yields satire; defined man is the focus and butt of the intellectual energies of the age in which he began to emerge, the Augustan. And that age's most engaging fiction is the man who is defined precisely by his disorientation, the man who has been installed (we all are) in the wrong universe, and stubbornly copes, and stubbornly declines to be surprised. His inventors called him the Man of Sense. Charles Babbage, we shall see, was his sturdy incarnation. In Buster Keaton, the automated man, he comes to full flower (they are iron petals).

II

The Man of Sense as Buster Keaton

Buster Keaton's face has been ranked "almost with Lincoln's as an early American archetype." He was the comedian of archaic dignity, its Aeschylus and its Scriblerus. If between archaic dignity and the comic there exists some hidden but necessary connection, we cannot better begin to understand what it is than by inspecting that face. "It was haunting," James Agee wrote, "haunting, handsome, almost beautiful, yet it was irreducibly funny; he improved matters by topping it off with a deadly horizontal hat, as flat and thin as a phonograph record. One can never forget Keaton wearing it, standing erect at the prow as his little boat is being launched. The boat goes grandly down the skids and, just as grandly, straight on to the bottom. Keaton never budges. The last you see of him, the water lifts the hat off the stoic head and it floats away."[1]

This is the true Art of Sinking, into which no one ever went so deeply as he. It is quintessential. If we are haunted

1. James Agee, *Agee on Film*, N. Y., 1958, 15.

by analogies with Wordsworth, we shall find no apposite quotation. Wordsworth dips only to recover again; over no sunken grandeur of his do the waters close majestically for ever. Yet whatever quality it is in Keaton's stoical descent that calls to mind so great a poet, both his habitual grandeur and his lapses, is a quality that has become available to the mind within the past three centuries, to be brought to apotheosis in the silent motion picture of the 1920's.

Kinesis was the rhetoric of that decade, when Americans did with pure motion what the English did about 1600 with language, and the French about 1880 with color. For those few years, before American eyes, the Newtonian universe flowered like a languid rose, disclosing, before its petals dropped away, all its intricate repertory of action, reaction, equilibrium. Man and machine, in that enchanted truce, meet nearly as equals.

You could understand how a thing worked by looking at it. A locomotive, a steam shovel, Calvin Coolidge, hid nothing from the mind; they did not require to be explained as all subsequent technology has required endlessly to be explained. (What does the eye tell us about a transistor radio?) Trajectories Everyman intuited with ease, and the Parallelogram of Forces irradiated his mind as Love does an angel's. The collaboration between audience and kinetic mime was nearly ideal. No one had trouble understanding how a snagged log with Buster clinging to its end could pivot up like a mast and then out over a waterfall's lip like a bowsprit; nor why, swinging down from its end on a rope to rescue the girl, he launched himself not toward her but away from her; nor by what con-

Abraham Cowley Counterfeits an Ode

version of potential to kinetic energy he is carried up, having snatched her from her ledge, exactly to that handy shelf of rock.[2] And this was not faked shot by shot. It was simply enacted and photographed.

Yet sometimes, somehow, glacially, the silent laws turn inimical: as when the boat, on its towrope, emerging from the basement, wholly demolishes the house; as when the champagne bottle dents its hull; as when, having gone down the ways, it continues to go down until only Keaton's hat remains afloat. At the end of another picture that hat alone—no words, no dates, no eulogy—is limned on his tombstone; as bleak a *siste viator* as the lines with which Wordsworth ended *Michael*.

Some silent nemesis beset Wordsworth also; and the same austerities of diction and syntax that yielded "She Dwelt among Untrodden Ways" and "Tintern Abbey" betrayed him into

> The far-fetched worm with pleasure would disown
> The bed we give him, though of sofest down,

and

> In March, December and in July,
> 'Tis all the same with Harry Gill;
> The neighbours tell, and tell you truly,
> His teeth they chatter, chatter still,

and

>   . . . the precious child,
> Which, after a short time, by some mistake
> Or indiscretion of the Father, died.

2. Sequence from *Our Hospitality*, 1923. See Rudi Blesh, *Keaton*, N. Y., 1966, 230.

Other poets, Keaton-wise, have been betrayed as well, just when their demeanor was most edifying. This strange event has happened so often that connoisseurs have classified a good many instances. The standard compendium is the anthology called *The Stuffed Owl*, which D. B. Wyndham Lewis and Charles Lee edited in 1930, a book invaluable to students of the seventeenth century. Unfortunately, its editors were less interested in their subject than in stylish sublimations of their impulse to snigger, so that what they were really documenting is seldom noticed. Their hidden subject was one of the most curious phenomena in the history of literature, the emergence of a new style so radical in its assumptions that it brought with it out of the void from which it came a wholly new way for poetry to fail, so that failure becomes a kind of positive quality. This is transcendental: it is as if someone could invent a new sin.

The editors of *The Stuffed Owl* came tantalizingly close to formulating this event; to read their preface is like watching Galileo fail to discover gravitation. They announce, for instance, their decision to begin this Anthology of Bad Verse with Cowley, for it turns out that when earlier producers of Bad Verse are bad, "they are tiresome to a degree. Cowley is the last poet of the Metaphysical School and about the first to be bad comically, and therefore makes a convenient jumping-off point."[3]

Let us rewrite that sentence. "Cowley is the first poet of the Augustan School, of whose procedures a novel byproduct is comic badness." Something happened late in the seventeenth century which *made possible* strikingly,

3. Lewis and Lee, *The Stuffed Owl*, N. Y., Capricorn Books, 1962, xix.

comically, transcendentally bad verse. One would like to be able to say what this was.

We are concerned not with semi-literacy but with the unaccountable lapses of serious poets: poets, let us say, sufficiently professional to look Buster Keaton in the face, who can yet address for instance an apostrophe to the "Spade! With which Wilkinson hath tilled his lands." Let us postulate that the bad verse of such a poet is *verse which has been published by mistake*. It has deceived its author, whose mind, fixed on some other quality, supposed it good, and it has continued to deceive him throughout the process of revision, of reading his composition to friends, of sending it to the printer, of reading proof, and inspecting the finished volume. And yet he is an author of some taste, some experience, some sensibility, who has proved his claim to these qualifications by publishing on other occasions good verse. It is clear that when this can happen the criteria for good verse have become exceedingly elusive. We remember Dr. Johnson's statement that verse is easily written; he spoke of walking up and down in his room and making fifty lines at a time; "the great difficulty," he told Boswell, "is to know when you have made good ones." For somehow sureness of taste has become the only, and a slippery, criterion for virtues by their very nature elusive. This has nothing to do with the excision of dullness. Dull writing has never deceived anyone, not even its author. He is not deceived in finding it interesting, he is merely interested in it. Another person need not be.

If Cowley was the first poet to risk an enterprise in which all depends on sureness of taste, and did not always manifest that sureness, it was not because he was the last Metaphysical poet but because he was the first Augustan. Johnson, who found him ridiculous, has discouraged us from thinking of him as an Augustan, indeed from thinking of him at all, except as a joke. For Johnson's successors the poet Milton admired was an unread joke; for ourselves, he is perhaps the ox we sacrifice to the shade of Donne. It is not for his "metaphysical" habits that we find him in *The Stuffed Owl*. In *The Stuffed Owl* he fits comfortably with his successors, not his predecessors; with the eighteenth and nineteenth century practitioners of the art of bathos. Here is one of the two extracts by which the editors illustrate his talent in this mode:

> Coy Nature (which remain'd, though agèd grown,
> A beauteous virgin still, enjoy'd by none,
>   Nor seen unveil'd by any one),
> When Harvey's violent passion she did see,
>   Began to tremble and to flee,
> Took sanctuary, like Daphne, in a tree:
> There Daphne's lover stopt, and thought it much
>   The very leaves of her to touch,
> But Harvey, our Apollo, stopt not so,
> Into the bark and root he after her did go. . . .
> What should she do? through all the moving wood
> Of lives endow'd with sense she took her flight;
> Harvey pursues, and keeps her still in sight.
> But as the deer long-hunted takes a flood,
> She leapt at last into the winding streams of blood;
> Of man's Meander all the purple reaches made,
>   Till at the heart she stay'd,
>   Where, turning head, and at a bay,
> Thus, by well-purgèd ears, was she o'erheard to say:
> "Here sure shall I be safe," said she;
> "None will be able sure to see
>   This my retreat, but only He
>   Who made both it and me.

Citizen Marx and Mr. Babbage Observed in Their Courses

> The heart of man, what art can e'er reveal?
>   A wall impervious between
>   Divides the very parts within,
> And doth the heart of man e'en from itself conceal."
>   She spoke, but ere she was aware,
>   Harvey was with her there. . . .

This is exquisitely ludicrous, and Cowley did not think it was. Johnson has taught us to see in such a passage the decadent Metaphysical manner, yoking together by violence heterogeneous ideas. But it is not really the "conceits" that make the trouble. They are not even conceits in Donne's sense at all. They are frantically logical developments of ideas a prose exposition could make perfectly acceptable. Sir Thomas Browne, for instance, could have paraphrased that passage with utter decorum. What makes them ridiculous is the rhetoric of the Grand Style. For verse is supposed to present prose sense with a heightened decorum, the heightened decorum that is later to become Matthew Arnold's "high seriousness." It requires that the poet climb onto a pedestal, so that we can tell he is writing poetry.

That is what comes of the Restoration emphasis on clarity; it leaves nothing whatever for the poet to do but strike a bardic posture and elevate his language. Language has only one function, to communicate information, and only one indispensable virtue, to be clear. Cowley is on all occasions a poet of absolute clarity. We see perfectly well why Nature is called "a beauteous virgin." He tells us why: she is "enjoy'd by none, nor seen unveil'd by any one." We can tell, if we know something of Harvey's researches, why in fleeing from his determined scrutiny Nature should first take refuge in a tree (where sap circulates, like blood), and hence why she should be compared to Ovid's Daphne. We can see why she takes refuge in a stream, since she has just been compared to a hunted deer, and hunted deer take refuge in streams; and why the streams should be streams of blood the theme of the poem makes perfectly clear; and how blood should introduce the inscrutability of the heart of man needs explaining to no one; and since it was he who penetrated the mysteries of the blood, and so of the heart, why, Harvey "was with her there."

Observe that when you are perpetually diagramming the reasonableness of what you are doing, it is open to any reader who has not fallen under the spell to wonder why you should be doing it at all. The danger posed by such a reader would seem to have been one of Dryden's principal discoveries, for Dryden began in the manner of Cleveland and finished more or less in the manner of Racine, having mastered the trick of substituting for figures of thought, where he can be as luckless as Cowley, what can only be called figures of tone, declaiming with unique authority resonant commonplaces:

> All human things are subject to decay,
> And when Fate summons, monarchs must obey.
> This Flecknoe found, who like Augustus, young
> Was call'd to empire, and had govern'd long.

This is Dryden's mock-heroic manner, and it is indistinguishable from his heroic manner. He goes on:

> In prose and verse, was own'd, without dispute,
> Thro' all the realms of *Nonsense*, absolute.

If for "Nonsense" we were to substitute some oriental name, we might suppose that we had before us a fragment of one of Dryden's heroic dramas. Dryden may be said to stare down the dangers of high seriousness; and in abandoning, to the extent that he did abandon it, the elaborately rationalized comparison, he established a mode which is only superficially less dangerous than Cowley's. For it depended on a sense of theatre as sure as Dryden's own, and whoever lacks that sure sense will repeatedly encounter disaster.

It was Pope in turn who discovered how ineffably comic such disaster could be. He was responsible for the mock treatise on *The Art of Sinking in Poetry*, the title of which implies, with a glance at Longinus, that what poetry is supposed to do is Rise, and the thesis of which is that falls, occurring as they do so much oftener than ascents, must be secured by some special technique which he undertakes to codify for us. He does not omit to quote some wondrous examples, for instance the glimpse of the Almighty as cosmic butler—

> He measures all the drops with wondrous skill,
> Which the black clouds, his floating Bottles, fill

—which two centuries later was to find its way into *The Stuffed Owl*. But it is notable that Pope himself, the most daring and far-ranging of eighteenth century poets, does not once tempt the Owl's editors. Yet every technique which he ridicules in *The Art of Sinking* and in *The Dunciad* is in his own poetry, for they are the only techniques that there are; and the price of poetry, he was almost alone in understanding, has come to be eternal vigilance. Pope used the bad verse of others as Flaubert was to use his *Dictionary of Received Ideas*, as a huge commonplace book on which his own creative enterprise could draw, building crazy edifices of congruous and incongruous simile, climax and anticlimax, low and heroic diction, which wobble majestically on their pivots without ever toppling off. In *The Art of Sinking* (1727) he defines "The Alamode Style," which is "fine by being new," and draws its images from "the present Customs and best Fashions of our Metropolis"; and one of his four examples is Nathaniel Lee's metaphor, conceived in 1676, for two armies on the point of engaging:

> Yon armies are the *Cards* which both must play;
> At least come off a *Saver* if you may:
> *Throw boldly* at the *Sum* the Gods have *set;*
> These on your side will all their fortunes *bet.*

Yet in 1714 he had himself expanded that very figure into the most brilliant seventy lines in *The Rape of the Lock.*

The same paper, the same ink, the same design, will earn one man, working for the Bureau of Engraving and Printing, his salary, and another, working for his art, hanging space in museums, and another, working for the mob, twenty years at Leavenworth. Work has no inherent virtue; it is valued as it is aimed. A producer about to release a silent movie exploiting dislike of the Kaiser was caught by the 1918 armistice; but transformed it into a marketable comedy by cutting out all the titles that denoted spoken words, and substituting others. Material has no inherent genre, it will tip in any direction. Lee's warfare tersely likened to a card game is absurd; Pope's card game elaborately likened to a clash of armies is exquisite. Analogies have no inherent decorum, their efficacy is a function of detailed judgment.

For poet and reader alike are now men of Judgment,

collaborating in that strange attempt to rear a whole civilization upon taste. Fine shades of congruity and incongruity must be distinguished with instinctive sureness. There is literally nothing that will not help sustain a poem, precisely as a satellite is maintained in orbit by forces whose intent, unbalanced, is to plunge it off into the infinite abyss forever. To move naturally amid such forces requires a training as rigorous as an astronaut's, and Horace, whose near-prose the Augustans found so congenial, compares the poet to the tight-rope walker:

> ille per extentum funem mihi posse videtur
> ire poeta, meum qui pectus inaniter angit[4]

—and Horace himself may be walking such a rope, or thinking of more than one kind of poet, since he has just been deploring gaudy spectacles, and expresses the idea of poetic fictions by a word *(inaniter)* which normally means "empty." One appreciates his nearly Keatonian reserve, much as one does Pope's intricate dealings with the same Epistle ("To Augustus"), line after line of bland insult which some admirers of George II applauded as wholesome panegyric. We shall be giving that Epistle more attention. Let us note meanwhile that poetry has become something you *appreciate* (instead of submitting, in the old way, to having your breast stirred *inaniter*), precisely because its success is so precarious; and consider the applicability of another of James Agee's evocations: Keaton's pictures, he remarks in a brilliant Newtonian simile, "are like a transcendent juggling act in which it seems that the whole universe is in exquisite flying motion and the one

4. Horace, *Epistles* II. i. 210-211. "It's as if he could walk on a tight-rope, the poet who can work me up over nothing."

point of repose is the juggler's effortless, uninterested face."[5]

The heroic and the mock-heroic have become one thing. Though Pope learned the resources of the English heroic while he was translating Homer, he had the sense not to attempt it when Homer was not there to protect him. Not merely Homer's schema of effects, but Homer's very reputation, is a part of Pope's *Iliad,* one of its balancing forces. How strange a poem it would seem had there been no Homer, and had Pope, in a periwigged England, simply made it all up! In *The Dunciad* subsequently, where there is no Homer, Pope writes with deliberate precariousness, enjoying as he had not in his *Iliad* the full virtuosity of his epic effects, secure in the knowledge that he is doing with taste, judgment, and a keen sense of the ridiculous exactly that which the Dunces do all the time. The follies he mimes of duncery are the dashing risks of excellence. You take your life in your hands when you move a step; for if the single pace of a man walking be analyzed, by snapshot, into fifty successive phases, not more than one or two of these, perhaps not any, will be inherently stable.

Newton's calculus implies this kind of analysis of anything moving, a planet, a pedestrian, or a poem. The reduction of such intuitions to sensate demonstration invariably takes a long time; it was not until 1887 that Muybridge's serial photographs of horses trotting and women climbing stairs supplied a visual equivalent.[6] The intelligence of Pope had grasped, however, by 1711 the principle

5. Agee, 15.
6. Eadweard Muybridge, *Animal Locomotion*, 1887. For selected reproductions see his *The Human Figure in Motion*, N. Y., 1955.

inherent in Newton's analysis of motion, that its swing is through numerous points of disequilibrium. That is why, as he tells us in the *Essay on Criticism,* "those move easiest who have learned to dance." It is also why a judgment which focuses on parts is almost sure to be mistaken. Though poems, like parabolae, invite analytic subdivision (paragraphs, couplets, lines, half-lines, syllables), we are to

> Survey the WHOLE, nor seek slight faults to find
> Where Nature moves, and Rapture warms the Mind.

He still, in 1711, speaks of faults, but they are perhaps discontinuities imposed by the analysis. By the time he has finished translating Homer he will be in a position to doubt if there be such things as faults which a correctly calculated movement cannot meaningfully incorporate. When he incorporates into *The Dunciad* one of his ludicrously apt similes—

> Like buoys, that never sink into the flood,
> On Learning's surface we but lie and nod

—he has achieved, and bent to the uses of his poem, a detail which might have occurred to some fumbling heroic dramatist, and which, had he encountered it in such a dramatist, he would have felt justified in placing on view in *The Art of Sinking.* He learned the way of his comic effects—

> And China's earth receives the smoking tide

(said of tea entering cups) from the high seriousness that was going on all around him. The only difference ("Survey the whole") is in the trajectory in which that line is one moment, a trajectory whose generating forces are the solemn ritual, the miniature means. What is *The Dunciad* itself, or what *The Rape of the Lock,* but a huge synthetic eighteenth century Stuffed Owl, confected with loving taxidermy out of the skins of a thousand sparrows?

Pope seems nowhere to refer to Newton's analytic strategies, but thought is guided by analogy, conscious or unconscious, and this was the accessible and sufficient analogy to prevent him from thinking of the poem as a whole which is the arithmetical sum of its parts, diminished by a small part, or as a chain made up of links, no stronger than its weakest link. No such old-fashioned analogies guide Pope's operations, as they still do Dryden's, who cannot risk a "bad" couplet. If Dryden found English brick and left it marble, he still thought of the poem as a building, reared in great blocks. What came to Pope as marble, however, he left as a system of tensions, limber, open, bending to the wind, like some Eiffel Tower of the imagination. It was, in subsequent decades, men still trying to elevate their language while iterating a prose sense, laying course upon course of great identical blocks, who left us a huge legacy of the unconsciously comic.

The Dunciad has another interesting quality: it is stuffed with Facts. Pope had a very sure sense of where to place these facts: he placed them in footnotes, to which such names as Bentley's were not uncommonly forged. His followers, and some of his predecessors, showed less judgment. One of the things that had happened to poetry since the Restoration was that Fact had arisen to bedevil it. This helps explain Cowley's troubles with the achievement of William Harvey, fitly to celebrate which required placing on record his awareness of a body of information, of a kind for dealing with which Homer and Pindar, who dealt in less specialized categories of praise and blame, really provide no precedent. That the human heart is imperviously divided into halves is a Fact: an isolated atom of knowledge, known only since Vesalius (1542), and not necessarily related to any other piece of knowledge or body of knowledge which we may happen to possess. And Cowley, unless he is going to praise Dr. Harvey in very general terms indeed, finds it necessary to amplify such information of this kind as he possesses, so that Nature must declaim how she will surely be safe within the heart of man, since

> A wall impervious between
> Divides the very parts within
>   And doth the heart of man e'en from itself conceal;

and Cowley no doubt feels that he has tucked his physiology into his rhetoric very gracefully.

For this tyranny of Fact the Royal Society was perhaps rather a mnemonic than a cause. Facts go with clarity, they go with clear and distinct ideas, they go with many other criteria of that age; that a society of learned men should have organized itself to celebrate Fact was part of the age's way of congratulating itself. And Sprat's Gulliverian theory of language, according to which words are simply names for things, and a proper style will be "a close, naked, natural way of speaking," that shall deliver "so many *things,* almost in an equal number of words," thus "bringing all things as near the Mathematical plainness, as they can,"[7] bespeaks not so much a respect for reality as an atomizing of reality into facts: so many things, innumerable things, as numerous as the little lexicographic

7. Thomas Sprat, *History of the Royal Society*, 1667, 112.

particles into which we have learned to atomize language.

Linguists became preoccupied with the word, and so with dictionaries where words are arranged without regard for their sense, in precisely the same way that writers became preoccupied with facts: for the fact is the atom of knowledge as the word is the atom of language. It was proposed that the taxonomy of facts should be mimed by signs comparably related, and the interactions of facts by systems regulating the intercourse of those signs, existing languages being all mauled by usage and deformed by the imperfect understanding of fact which hampered their first framers. In 1668 John Wilkins published his *Essay towards a Real Character and a Philosophical Language*, complete with a transcription of the Lord's Prayer into orderly pothooks. Others, including Newton, busied themselves with such schemes, but none proved appealing. What *was* achieved on this front was the restructuring of English, in the course of a few decades, as a synthetic language, a derivative of which we still write. That this is not too strongly put anyone may convince himself who will compare, say, Jacobean prose with Augustan: into the reconstitution of the mother tongue flowed, finally, the innovating energies that had tried for a while to fabricate, after rational principles, what was to have been mankind's first tidy instrument of registration. Registration, not discourse: the most profound innovation of Royal Society Prose was this, that the relation of subject to predicate was no longer something affirmed, by a speaker, but something verified, by an observer. The man speaking, the Donne, the Herbert, recedes, then vanishes. He is replaced by the perceiving consciousness.

In a virtually new language, stylistic principles had to be rediscovered from scratch. It is not surprising that many experiments were unlucky. Bishop Sprat himself composed a poem "On His Mistress Drowned," in which he apostrophized a stream and noted with accuracy that its movement was indivisible:

> Sweet stream, that dost with equal pace
> Both thyself fly, and thyself chase . . .

from which we know that he has looked at a stream, and thought about a stream, and considered analytically its motion, instead of taking the mere poetical idea of a stream uninspected from the annals of literature. Yet *The Stuffed Owl* claims him; for he insists on writing out this observation in verse, which implies the rhetoric of one who feels and speaks, and hence the emotional or ethical importance of whatever its speaker has observed.

By Dr. Johnson's time appalling verse was concerning itself with nothing but facts, and facts raised to a rhetorical pitch (prose sense with a heightened decorum); so that when Johnson heard of Dyer's *The Fleece* he announced, "The subject, Sir, cannot be made poetical. How can a man write poetically of serges and druggets!" And James Grainger wrote *The Sugar-Cane, a Poem*, of which Johnson asked, "What could he make of a sugar-cane? One might as well write 'The Parsley-bed, a Poem'; or 'The Cabbage-garden, a Poem.' " It was Grainger who had the ill-luck to epitomize the intractability of Fact, when he commenced a paragraph "Now, Muse, let's sing of *Rats*," and did not deceive Boswell into supposing that he had effected any improvement when, this apostrophe being greeted with mirth, he later changed "rats" to "the whisker'd vermin race."[8]

Yet Fact, despite such misadventures, will not die; it continues to creep up the slopes of Parnassus like crab grass, and it is finally Wordsworth, of all people, who is the very alembicator of Fact. No other poet is at such pains to assure us, over and over, of the absolute veracity of all his affirmations. Of an elegiac poem on his brother, he informs us that it was "composed near the Mountain track that leads from Grasmere through Grisdale Hawes, where it descends toward Paterdale." This is pertinent information, because the poem[9] contains the words "Here did we stop"; and we are to rest assured that "here" means "here," on the very spot where these words, long afterward, are being written. And should anyone desire to check the geography of the third stanza, the very spot is still more particularly identified: "the point is two or three yards below the outlet of Grisdale tarn, on a foot-road by which a horse may pass to Paterdale—a ridge of Helvellyn on the left, and the summit of Fairfield on the right." And as for the plant from which, in the same poem, his last comfort is derived, we are not to relegate it to some fanciful poetic catalogue, with "the rath primrose, that forsaken dies," or "cowslips wan that hang the pensive head": no, we are given, in a note, its common name, Moss Campion, and its Linnaean binomial, *silene acaulis*.

The place for such assurances, here as in *The Dunciad*, is at the foot of the page; there are notorious instances of the havoc they can wreak by climbing up into the poem,

8. Boswell, *Life of Johnson*, March 21, 1776.
9. "Elegiac Verses in Memory of my Brother, John Wordsworth."

as when Wordsworth gives us the dimensions of a pond, three feet long by two feet wide, and assures us, in iambic tetrameter, that he has measured it from side to side, whether with his walking-stick or with a folding ruler he does not say.[10] It is clear that he feels haunted by a sense of responsibility toward mere data; nor would he have us suppose him insensible to the primary function of the real language of men, which is to convey information. But the decorum of the factual is comic, because one can never tell from what direction a new fact may impinge. The invention of Fact, early in the seventeenth century, evoked within fifty years the invention of that indomitably comic contrivance the novel, the function of which is to incorporate a random fusillade of information into a loose system, propelled forward by narrative, the data as they accumulate moving steadily forward into a vacuum of expectation. Wordsworth seems unaware of the uses of the novel, though he has a dim sense that narrative is relevant to his problems, and rarely attempts a poem of any length without a narrative framework. For him the problem posed by facts was that of the relevant tone for introducing them: the problem, in short, of how a person, who is taking the trouble to speak, may be related to a body of data which represents no trouble and no passion, but is simply *there*. He is the last eminent imitator, the last until Buster Keaton, of that eighteenth century paladin The Man of Sense, who moved through his world beset by the unsleeping perils of the ridiculous.

This figure throve on the Grandeur of Generality. It

10. "The Thorn." Wordsworth subsequently eliminated this detail.

was written of him that he knew enough of the world to undervalue it, and went to heaven with a very good mien.[11] Pope noted that he approved what the foolish were so naive as to admire, and Pope's line in turn seems indebted to a translation of La Bruyère that was current in his boyhood, where we are informed of the Man of Sense that he "has in him the Seeds of all Truths and all Sentiments, nothing is new to him. He admires little, He approves."[12] He is not the polymath, not the Renaissance virtuoso. He is incarnate equilibrium, the man who cannot be surprised. He belongs at the still point of a stable world; he is a fiction, of course; he is the age's conspiracy to pretend to itself that the world is indeed stable. By Wordsworth's time he was already an anachronism; by Byron's, more bizarre or more aggressive strategies seemed called for, and the Man of Sense had outlived his usefulness except as a comic persona.

For the world had never, all that time, been stable; the Man of Sense was invented at about the time when it grew clear how the world, far from rocking amid majestic commonplaces, teemed with empirical novelty, with Facts. It was by these that the Man of Sense was determined not to be surprised. Behold him, then, groping across his scarred plain, while bullets, each one a neutral, lethal datum, whiz above his head. These bullets are messages from the sensate universe, all that there is to experience. The plain, not something to experience but a ground merely

11. *The Tatler*, No. 5 (1709), as quoted in F. R. Leavis, *Revaluation*, N. Y., 1963, 138-9.
12. See the note to line 391 of his "Essay on Criticism" in Pope, *Pastoral Poetry and an Essay on Criticism*, ed. Audra and Williams, New Haven, 1961, 284.

there as memories are there, is that world to which man was once able to know he belonged, above the brutes, a little lower than the angels, between the earthly and the heavenly city, crowned with glory and honor. The sun and moon in their dance saluted it once, the Hyades carried its water, and Hesper hung in the night its evening star. It was then, when man was first generating sentences, a habitable actuality; later for John Donne, when the New Philosophy had called all in doubt, a substantial though waning hypothesis. Donne in 1611 can still think of facts as random though unnerving curiosities. A century later nothing but their interlaced trajectories can be seen filling the air. And amid this fusillade our Man of Sense, dogmatically refusing to be surprised, is Royal Society Man, perpetually making notes, glancing at his chronometer as his hat is carried away, or (determined to maintain "the sublime" in the old sense) rising upright and inviting the Muse to sing of these facts: of the sugar-cane, of the wool industry, of mensuration, of circumspection, of Rats. Refusal to be surprised, it will later appear, is an indomitably comic posture, as in the White Knight; two centuries more, and a comedian of genius will bring it to apotheosis, in study after study of moral imperturbability trapped by mechanism. James Agee once more, transcribing from a Keaton film, provides us with a terminal vision of the Man of Sense: "Trapped in the side wheel of a ferry-boat, saving himself from drowning only by walking, then desperately running, inside the accelerating wheel like a squirrel in a cage, his only real concern was, obviously, to keep his hat on."[13]

13. Agee, 16.

III

The Counterfeiters

Buster Keaton's subject was kinetic man, a being he approached with the almost metaphysical awe we reserve for a Doppelgänger. This being was, eerily, himself, played by himself, then later in a projection room, watched by himself: an experience never possible to any generation of actors in the previous history of the world. He could watch himself, moreover, doing again things that in much earlier phases of his life he had actually done: being blown about by a cyclone, for instance, as he was in Kansas at the age of two and one-half. And his father in more than one film *was* his father, Joe Keaton, and the bride he plucked off the ledge near the waterfall was indeed his bride of two years, Natalie Talmadge Keaton, between whose life and his own he already felt sundering forces as implacable as tons of descending water.[1]

Keaton's great creative period was 1921-1927, the age of *Ulysses* and "The Hollow Men." In being his own subject he was equally Joyce's and Eliot's contemporary. More Keaton films than one—for instance *The Playhouse, Daydreams* and *Sherlock Jr.*—might almost be subtitled

1. Rudi Blesh, *Keaton*, N. Y., 1966, 221-222.

portraits of the artist as a young man, with a complexity of symbolic displacement hardly to be matched in the auto-inspection of earlier craftsmen. "A Portrait of the Artist as a Young Man" (1484) meant that the thirteen-year-old Albrecht Dürer had spent an afternoon investigating the way of bringing together what he knew about drawing and what he could see in a mirror. "Artist," in that time of innocent looking, was simply a word to designate the sitter for an exercise which might on a different afternoon have been performed with the artist's cat. Dürer the craftsman sees nothing particularly mysterious in Dürer's face, though there is much that is mysterious in his ability to draw it.

Rembrandt rather more than a century later takes more interest in the fact that he is looking at himself. When Rembrandt does "A Portrait of the Artist as a Young Man," his attention is divided between the marks time has placed on that face since it last gazed out of a mirror, and the visible tokens, around the eyes and mouth, of something in which Dürer seems to have taken less interest: this man's unique mysterious selfhood. There is no sign however that he is engrossed, or means us to fathom his engrossment, in the face of a unique *type* of man, the creative physiognomy. He is a unique man, only that, and each of us is. What he invites us to study is a face, Rembrandt's face, but not an artist's face. He is a craftsman, like Dürer; but beyond Dürer, meditating on the transiencies of being also a man.

The next famous *Portrait of the Artist as a Young Man* is not a picture but a book. The title goes out of its way to suggest analogies with a picture, while the very last line on the last page, the pair of dates, stresses divergences. Far from reproducing the conditions of Dürer's afternoon with his own face or his cat's, this book was written between 1904 and 1914, while the author was aging from twenty-two to thirty-two, and concerns itself with a subject like-wise in continual transit, from babyhood to the age of about twenty. The mirror, if mirror there be, is the mirror of memory, and what appears in it is a being called The Artist. We are shown what The Artist is like when he is a young man, whether the artist's name be Joyce or Wilde or Shelley or Spender or Poe, though probably not Dürer or Rembrandt: the scope of the word "artist" had been suddenly much enlarged a few decades before Joyce's birth.

We are told that the artist as a young man is different from other young men, because he is a different sort of being. Indeed he may grow so preoccupied with that differ-ence that he will never produce any art, as a look at Stephen Dedalus may suggest. When his difference has been prop-erly validated, Joyce suggests that it resembles a priest's vocation, and his job will be to act as "a priest of the eternal imagination, transmuting the daily bread of experience into the radiant body of everliving life."[2] Those of us who consume that body (and Joyce, surely by no accident, speaks in *Finnegans Wake* of his readers as consumers) will presumably derive from the transmuted experience benefits not obtainable from the experience in its uncon-secrated state, when we perhaps merely lived it, just as

2. Joyce, *Portrait of the Artist as a Young Man*, v. The phrase passes through Stephen's mind while he is composing his *villanelle*.

the bread which has been transubstantiated in the priest's hands feeds the soul though formerly it was fit only to feed the body. This gives us reasons for tolerating and feeding the artist, differences and all, and reasons similar to the ones Catholic Dublin gave for tolerating and feeding its innumerable priests, who were also pretty unsettling company, and contributed quite as little as does the artist to the health of Dublin's economy.

A priest, then, changing everything but the appearance of what he handles: it seems a thoroughly Romantic formulation. Prophet, priest and king, these were the three heads of the Romantic Cerberus, and Romantic orthodoxy treated them as counterfeit and usurping artists. The Shelleyan artist, trumpet who sang to battle and unacknowledged legislator of the world, unites the roles of prophet and king, while Joyce, who disliked battles and had looked at legislators with a colder eye than Shelley's, evoked in still more deliberate metaphor the third member of that triad, the artist-priest. But lest the metaphor date with the fading of priest, along with prophet and king, from symbolic potency, Joyce linked artist-priest with another formulation, nearly three centuries in preparation: the artist-counterfeiter.

For Stephen goes forth to forge in the smithy of his soul the uncreated conscience of his race, and Joyce glosses the verb "forge" when Stephen reappears in *Finnegans Wake* rechristened Shem the Penman, a name drawn from a Victorian melodrama about a forger.[3] Shem's chronicler

3. J. S. Atherton, *The Books at the Wake*, N. Y., 1960, 70.

goes so far as to call *Ulysses* "an epical forged cheque on the public,"[4] and we are only beginning to realize how thoroughly counterfeit is the *Portrait* itself, that book which passed so long as autobiography. The hellfire sermon, for instance, was not something Joyce heard in the chapel but something he bought from a pamphlet-rack.[5] Though the union of forger and priest may reflect Joyce's doubts about what actually happens when the words are spoken over the sacramental bread, it is generally better, in examining his meanings, to keep his personal history out of mind. He saw very deeply into what interested him, and in linking the functions of priest and forger freed his thought from his mere time, his mere Shelleyan afflatus, and brought it to the heart of anything an artist does. The artist makes something that is like something else, and yet, not being the thing that it is like, exudes a magic to which, whatever our sophistication, we can never grow really indifferent. All art, from a time before the bulls in the cave at Lascaux, comes from magical beginnings about which we vainly guess. The Aurignacian draftsman, like the sculptor at Luxor, may have been a kind of priest and was certainly a kind of forger.

And as the forge of Dedalus has become in modern times the skill of the penman, so the artist, who used to make things that were wanted, like a blacksmith, has come to make things we cannot think why we want, such as reproductions of Campbell's soup tins. Yet we accept them, because Art consecrates them. Hence arises what

4. *Finnegans Wake*, N. Y., 1939, 181.
5. *Hell Opened to Christians*, nineteenth century translation of a seventeenth century tract by G. P. Pinamonti, S.J. See J. R. Thrane's article in M. Magalaner, ed., *A James Joyce Miscellany, Third Series*.

connoisseurs of impasse will one day call the Warhol Situation, after Andy Warhol.

Warhol, who began by imitating soup labels with consummate skill, apparently contemplated a progress from painting to sculpture in emulation of his colleague Jasper Johns, who had turned out a Ballantine's beer can in solid bronze. This artifact, for which a large price was immediately paid, differs from its original, within the limits of the artist's skill, in only two particulars: it is much heavier, and it contains no beer. But Warhol cast no bronze. For it suddenly appeared that the Campbell Company, which up to that time had let us think that its business was to feed its customers and its stockholders, was actually engaged in a massive counterfeiting operation. It was flooding the supermarkets with cheap imitations of an Andy Warhol sculpture, and before the sculptor had so much as gotten to work. The entrepreneurs who deluge us with cheap Mona Lisas had at least the grace to wait until da Vinci had finished. Warhol in turn, having over da Vinci the advantage of being on the spot, was equal to the challenge of mass production. He took to carrying home from the supermarket dozens of these 17½-cent imitations, which he proceeded to autograph and place on sale at a price established, as all prices are, by the free market. This proved to be six dollars per can. It is clear that Mr. Warhol now has the Campbell Soup Company working for him, part time at least. It should also be clear that he has posed a neat epistemological problem. For the dream of Zeuxis, at whose painted grapes the birds pecked, is fulfilled at last; the gap between the artifact and the thing represented by the artifact seems virtually closed. It was a Greek dream, that Pygmalion's statue might be conceivably so lifelike it could start to move. Vaucanson's duck, a long stride in that direction, proves to have been no more than a middle term. For it is an American reality, that sculptured soup cans, complete with the sculptor's signature, will if punctured yield real soup.

According to the official theory of representational art, during every one of the twenty thousand years since the first bull was drawn on the wall of the first cave the creative imagination has labored to achieve this result, the artifact indistinguishable from its model. One would therefore expect sounds of hosannah from the custodians of this theory: at the very least, a testimonial dinner for Andy Warhol, jointly sponsored by the Anglo-Saxon press and the theoreticians of socialist realism, the main course perhaps soup instead of peacock. We hear instead ungrateful mutterings. Pygmalion, it is alleged, had to make his statue, whereas Warhol did not make his soup tins. It is difficult to be impressed by this argument. If Pygmalion's statue was in bronze, as important Greek statues were, then it was made at the foundry, as Rodin's were. Rubens operated a factory so skilled it would be difficult to prove he ever touched a brush to numerous paintings conventionally called his, the work of the great nineteenth century illustrators Doré and Tenniel is known to us by way of engravings not a line of which they executed, and Alexandre Dumas père with his loft full of apprentices perfected the art of issuing whole novels without lifting a pen. No one can deny that the actual shaping of the artifact has frequently and without scandal been delegated to someone with more time or more skill or better facilities than

Two Houyhnhnms Consider If the Counterfeit
Intelligence Could Be, After All, a Yahoo

the man who conceived it, and if we are in search of a concern with the skill and facilities to execute perfect Campbell's Soup cans we need not look further than Mr. Warhol did.

The stubborn question remains, by what alchemy the Warhol signature transformed those tins into display pieces (and multiplied their value thirty-five-fold). We may not be able to find a better analogy than Joyce's; by the imposition of a signature, not yours or mine but someone's whom fame had already linked with soup labels, as by the utterance of words of consecration, not by you or by me but by someone duly ordained, the mere sensate thing undergoes a change which does not affect its physical or chemical properties in the slightest; yet collectors' money has been spent to testify that something has altered. It is even possible to designate that change: in the beginning was the Word, and from being an object the can became an utterance. It became a kind of statement by Andy Warhol. The signature did exactly what a signature does when an executive at Campbell's affixes his own to a letter composed by his secretary. The signature makes the letter a thing uttered by him. Previously it was a typographical doodle assembled out of quotations from other letters: dear sir, in reply to, on the other hand. So the signature on the soup tin transforms it from a mere item of commerce into a slight but irreducible, complex, somewhat facetious utterance having to do with the status of the artist, the nature of art, the autism of a culture that buys what it eats unseen and then looks at nothing it buys, photolithographed abundance, conspicuous nonconsumption, and the long history of artifact as counterfeit.

For we need not compose our utterances so long as we endorse them. There are moments to which only a quotation is adequate; and the soup can, signed, may be said to quote one phrase from the stuttering monologue of our beautifully adept machines. And Warhol's gesture in quoting quotes a gesture of Marcel Duchamp's, who about 1915 titled an ordinary snowshovel "In Advance of the Broken Arm," and placed it in an exhibition of sculpture.[6] And that deed had in its time a different meaning from Warhol's, since its context was not mass-produced abundance but a floundering strife against snow. Both artists invited men to look at some common thing seldom looked at, but the meaning of each invitation is inflected by the context in which it is issued, including the context of all the artist's work. Warhol is prodigal, Duchamp so reticent that his *oeuvre* has been compared to "a chessboard on which each pawn occupies a strategic position," which "explains the rarity of the moves and the impossibility of repetition."[7] For the counterfeiter's gesture, in Duchamp's view, must *be* a gesture, not a way of life; otherwise it becomes not a comment on reduplication (as the ting of the triangle comments on orchestral blather) but an alternative reality, banal as the one it began by teasing. Warhol, more daring, competes with abundance; how many soup tins has he autographed? And what happens if a signature is tampered with?

For consider the plight of Nathanael West, who proposed to demonstrate the absurdity of the civilization that

6. R. Lebel, *Marcel Duchamp*, N. Y., 1959, 168. Since the original is lost, any exhibited version is a replica, i.e., a different snow shovel.
7. Lebel, 96.

generated the Horatio Alger phenomenon, by contriving yet more absurd extensions of Algerian citations; reading for instance in *Andy Grant's Pluck*

> "What pay do you get?" he asked.
> "Five dollars a week."
> "I get seven, but it's too small. A man can't live on it. Why, my car-fare costs me sixty cents a week."

and writing in *A Cool Million*

> "How much do you get?" was the forward youth's next question.
> "Thirty dollars a week and found," said Lem, honestly.
> "I get thirty-five without keep, but it's too little for me. A man can't live on that kind of money, what with the opera once a week and decent clothes. Why, my carfare alone comes to over a dollar, not counting taxicabs."

West earned for his pains the reproof that "literary echoes" damaged *A Cool Million* "irreparably;"[8] and yet the unchallengeable strategy would have been to use *Andy Grant's Pluck* as Duchamp used the snowshovel, copying it out verbatim but signing it "Nathanael West."

Or imagine a procedural excerpt from a marriage manual, with appended to it the signature, Jonathan Swift.

Or an ennobling picture purporting to show "Stalin demonstrating to the Leningrad Academy of Sciences that $E = mc^2$": signed in Cyrillic characters, a routine idealization; with the signature, say, of Max Beerbohm, it would be something else.

8. The reproof and the evidence are both cited by Douglas H. Shepard, "Nathanael West Rewrites Horatio Alger Jr.," *Satire Newsletter*, Fall 1965, 13-28.

Like every other aspect of the Warhol Situation, the importance of the signature on the soup can points up problems that have been latent in the Western psyche ever since, in the seventeenth century, it slowly became aware of art as art. That awareness synchronized with, and may have been caused by, the ascendancy of empirical philosophies. And no sooner had the life of the mind begun to make a virtue of radical empiricism—which assumes that we are to discern things while pretending to ourselves that we do not know what they are—than two related consequences became inevitable. First, what the schoolmen used to call accidents, the skin of coherent appearances, became all that there was to know, since the senses stop at appearances and the rules of empiricism forbid the mind to leap past the senses. And secondly, works of the imagination became an impediment to orderly knowledge. It became quite clear for the first time that there existed, testifying to much human effort, a phenomenon called Poetry, consisting of statements not borne out by careful observation. Thus John Locke was forced to conclude that whereas the Judgment separates and classifies what the senses deliver, the poetic faculty, which he calls Fancy, can only blend and confuse, which is amusing but not enlightening.[9] Such playthings, in the childhood of the race, were understandable, but these times call for men of Judgment.

The response of the savants was to promote Longinus' treatise on the Sublime, which allows you to be poetic *and* factual, as when you announce that In the Beginning God Created the Heavens and the Earth; and the Earth was Without Form, and Void. That way stuffed owls lay. The

9. John Locke, *Essay Concerning Human Understanding*, II.xi.2.

response of the magicians, who since paleolithic times have had the imagination in their keeping, was characteristically direct. A fraternity who in various periods have disguised themselves as moralists, as flatterers, as church decorators, had now no difficulty in disguising themselves as men of judgment. And perceiving that the world in the man of judgment's head is an orderly counterfeit of the world by which his body is surrounded, they became counterfeiters. The first notable triumph of the new esthetics of fraud was The Life and Strange Surprising Adventures of Robinson Crusoe, written by Himself. It is a lucid, orderly work, devoid of those appurtenances we can no longer defend: fables, expressions drawn from ancient writers, excrescences of rhetoric. The word is attached to the object, not to "literature" nor to the adjacent word. The very savages are certified by anthropology. The flaw in this work seems almost too trivial to mention. It is merely that Robinson Crusoe never existed.

We have already seen how Counterfeitable Man came into existence, but there are three things still to understand about the act of the literary counterfeiter. What we have here, first of all, is *the book Robinson Crusoe would have written, if he had existed.* This follows directly from the primary dogma of empiricism, that our knowledge is not of things but of their traces. We can see the apple, but it may be wax; luckily we have a sense of taste as well. We can see the bear's footprint, but unless he is standing in front of us we cannot be sure about the bear. Our senses show us only marks in the clay, and some skillful person may have molded them. If you can have the footprint without the bear, you can also have Crusoe's *Life* without

Crusoe. Crusoe also saw a footprint, but could not usefully assume it was forged, since to postulate a forger is still to postulate a second man. The reader is meant to respond to Crusoe's book exactly as Crusoe responded to Friday's footprint. He is to assume that the system of reality accessible to him contains one more man than he had previously surmised.

Second, we have a sophisticated consequence of the empirical habit of detaching words from the persons who utter them. Words, the philosophers kept repeating, are labels we gum onto things; grammar is a set of rules for combining words, which ideally would imitate the combining properties of things; and a language is simply a (disorderly) collection of words and a (haphazard) set of rules, most deplorable but capable of being tidied up somewhat by method. Fictions, in the past, were generated by rhetorical artifice, that is, by some ferment within the language itself; but order does not ferment. So be it; we shall write out *Robinson Crusoe* fact by fact, and stuff it with catalogues of things all accurately named; word shall follow word as event would have followed event; and to what end? To this end, that the language will stubbornly coalesce not about these facts but about a person who does not exist.

And third, we see the folly of trying to explain away Warhol transubstantiating soup tins, or Picasso metamorphosing a toy car into a baboon's head, by protesting that magic is cheap and that the true artist is really a craftsman. The craftsman theory assumes that you know what the artist is going to do (translate Homer, or sculpt Queen Anne), and then watch closely to see how well he does it.

Of course the minute he does something unexpected he and the theorist are in separate but equal difficulties: he because he has lost touch with his public (a public trained not on art but on the theory), and the theorist because he has lost the use of his criteria, and carries on as though an invisible hand had removed his trousers. Such scandals are familiar. But the craftsman is never really under control even when his hand is moving as we expect. For to ask him to do what has been done before is to ask him to counterfeit something, and the counterfeiter is never doing what we think. We see him bent over his table, and imagine him bent on the manufacture of an object, resembling a twenty dollar bill as closely as his craftsmanship will permit. We suppose that his work is an exercise in craftsmanship. It is not. It is an exercise in creative metaphysics. What the counterfeiter is imitating is not the bill but the moment when that bill was (we are to suppose) issued by the Treasury of the United States: not a visible thing but an invisible event: perfectly invisible: it never happened. In the same way the logical term of Vaucanson's simulations was a nonexistent necessary egg.

This grows quite clear if we consider the Shakespearean forgeries of William Ireland (1777-1835), which passed for a while as true documents and high tragedy. He did not forge a play; he wrote a play; and he wrote a bad one. *Vortigern: a Tragedy* is *Vortigern: a Tragedy:* absurd and unreadable. What Ireland counterfeited was the (alleged) occasion on which those acts and scenes, those speeches and rhythms, were composed by William Shakespeare. The text is manufactured, as all texts are, with paper and ink. The created thing, so long as the forgery stands, is not the text but an incident in Shakespeare's biography. Ireland was really a kind of historical novelist.

In the same way Daniel Defoe (whom we have not hitherto mentioned, since it is more convenient to imagine him as amanuensis for the syndicate of magicians) wrote *Robinson Crusoe* but forged a book "by" Robinson Crusoe and counterfeited Robinson Crusoe himself. The counterfeiting went on all the time he was writing the book; the forgery occurred on the moment when he elected to omit his own name from the titlepage. In so slight a moment, as Adam learned, is the world altered. For to be told, poker-faced, that it is not the fabrication we would gladly accept, but the very thing that is normally fabricated—a memoir, a testimony—this somehow changes a book, even when we do not believe what we are being told about it. We shall be enquiring into that "somehow."

But let us first return, before we forget how it works, to the principle that counterfeit persons emerge from a language which theory has separated from its speakers. A commonplace of modern language theory, though a commonplace guarded by ferocious border skirmishing, holds that languages are the work of the people who speak them. But the eighteenth century, turned toward the taxonomy of objects, found a different notion persuasive: a language (once tidied up, more or less on the analogy of Latin) is an intricate, self-sufficient machine with which mere speakers should not be allowed to monkey, unless they have first mastered the instruction book. Turn where we will, we see lexicographers and grammarians hooshing the folk away, lest they strip syntactic gears or corrode with their fingermarks the polished surfaces meant to reflect a

A Franco-Cantabrian Muralist Invents Art

world. For the language, its parts classified in dictionaries and its workings clarified in grammars, is a model, as intricate as the mind finds necessary, of the intricate stable order of Creation. It is incarnate good sense; to master its workings is to be civilized; through a well-schooled mind, *it* speaks.

As the system of arithmetic contains all possible calculations, this system—call it L—contains all possible meaningful utterances: writings, rather, since only chirographic deliberation, immune to the shortcuts of gesture and intonation, can do it justice. No said thing—no function of L—will bear the impress of personality, any more than does the theorem of Pythagoras. The writer is not a person, he is the amanuensis of verity, who will only corrupt what he writes to the extent that he yields to passion, or shirks the discipline of objectivity.

But somehow that which is written implies a person, an A. Pope or an R. Crusoe. This person is a state L_1 of the system L, which contains him (he exists only among verbal configurations) and may be said to generate with a part of its mind the sentences proper to him. The entire language L is in fact a simulating device.[10] It can simulate, by specializing itself, any reasonable person we like: L_1, L_2, L_3 . . . L_n: the Modest Proposer, or Lemuel Gulliver, or the virtuoso who wrote *A Tale of a Tub* and also (he tells us) *A General History of Ears,* or the prosodist of a stolen lock of hair, or Pope's Homer for that matter, a highly correct suppositious poet who will not do simply

10. As is the Turing Machine, which suggested this analysis. Turing's simulator is explained in the next chapter. Donald Davie's conception of diction as a selection of language from which the poem's words are in turn selected is a special case of our principle.

anything with language, but only the things pertinent to his vast enterprise. Pope's Homer has this to say about the disobedient:

> Back to the skies with shame he shall be driv'n,
> Gash'd with dishonest wounds, the scorn of Heav'n:
> Or far, oh far from steep Olympus thrown,
> Low in the dark Tartarean gulf shall groan;
> With burning chains fix'd to the brazen floors,
> And lock'd by Hell's inexorable doors.

Shift the language however from state L_h to state L_r, and it commences to generate verses proper to the *Rape of the Lock:*

> Whatever spirit, careless of his charge,
> His post neglects, or leaves the fair at large,
> Shall feel sharp vengeance soon o'ertake his sins,
> Be stopp'd in vials, or transfix'd with pins;
> Or plunged in lakes of bitter washes lie,
> Or wedg'd whole ages in a bodkin's eye.[11]

The person simulated in L_h has a taste for terminal sonorities (thrown, groan, floors, doors) to which his L_r counterpart replies with a different sampling of the vowel scale (sins, pins, lie, eye). L_h for emphasis opens lines with trochees; L_r inclines to iambs. L_h has affinities with the system L_p, which some decades previously generated *Paradise Lost;* L_r with the system L_t, which generated *The Tempest.*

But this is idealized. These subsystems were not in fact generated by the system L, but only by so much of it as was carried in the understanding of Alexander Pope, whose Judgment these altered decorums illustrate. Pope would have explained the differences we have been no-

11. These passages are juxtaposed by Norman Callan, "Alexander Pope," in B. Ford, ed., *Pelican Guide to English Literature*, Harmondsworth, 1957, vol. iv, 260-261.

ticing by talking of a decorum of subject, to which the
language conforms. . . . But which Pope? The being of
jaunty rectitude who wrote the Epistle to Dr. Arbuthnot?
The long-clawed retaliator upon Lady Mary Wortley
Montague? The perfervid moralist of the *Essay on Man?*
The scatologist of *Dunciad II?* Given two poems, comparable in their adaptation of means to subject, it was a
staple of coffee-house speculation whether the same hand
had or had not written both. Shifting decorums in practice
imply shifting authorship, or one man imitating the ways
of many. It was Pope who found this principle so self-
evident that he supposed Shakespeare to have obeyed it,
venturing that if the names of the characters were sup-
pressed throughout the Folio, every speech could yet
unhesitatingly be assigned to its speaker. We who hear
Shakespeare's idiom throughout the plays are less sure
that he subdivided himself so systematically.

The model we have been proposing of how a Universal
Language works, generating subsystems which are quasi-
persons, has the merit of uniting several themes intuition
and history also unite, but exposition usually disjoins. We
shall see in the next chapter how readily it assimilates the
linguistic modes of simulation to the mechanical, and so
points forward to the Xerox machine and the engineer's
counterfeit brain. We have touched on its power to illu-
minate the Augustan insistence on Judgment and decorum.
We can see with its aid why satire should have been so
congenial a genre, since the man who commands L, or as
much of L as is relevant, can observe and exploit
the necessary limitations of his subsystem L_1, and can also
pretend, if censors grow inquisitive, that only L_1 exists,
not he. We can understand the puzzling blurring of Au-

gustan genres, the virtual coalescence for example of heroic and mock-heroic, since genres imply evaluations, imported only by persons, whereas the object-world and its model the system L are depersonalized alike, and L_d who seems to be writing *The Dunciad* only partly overlaps with L_p who held the pen. We can see the entire system tending toward Symbolism, a poetic of poems without authors, which make no affirmations and eschew personal colorations, but are generated, allegedly, by the autonomous language. We can understand the concern of non-symbolist poets—a Pope, a later Yeats, an Ezra Pound —for masks and personae. And we need not be puzzled by the Augustan affinity for citations, parodies and echoes. For the dead have been made into persons by time: we call Waller's book "Waller": and when we appropriate configurations they have used we can play the open neutrality of all language (the formulae are simply neat words in a neat order) against what all readers know a certain dead man to have "meant" by them. The most eminent modern exploiter of this method, T. S. Eliot, is also the most insistent formulator of homages to an inheritance, weightier than himself, called the Language ("A ceaseless care, a passionate and untiring devotion to language, is the first conscious concern of the poet"), and the achievement of many passages in *The Waste Land* is to make lines identical with lines Shakespeare or Webster wrote sound like lines Eliot might have written himself.

A remarkable story by Jorge Luis Borges[12] invites us to consider several pages of manuscript written, at the cost of unimaginable spiritual contortions, by a twentieth-cen-

12. "Pierre Menard, Author of the Quixote," in *Labyrinths*, N. Y., 1962.

tury Frenchman. These pages are identical word for word with several pages of *Don Quixote*, a work composed with considerably less trouble by a sixteenth-century Spaniard. And the Frenchman's pages, says Borges accurately, though literally identical with the Spaniard's are almost infinitely richer. As they are, so long as we see behind arranged words the act of a man finding and arranging them, and do not suppose that these words were simply copied. We have said that we cannot imagine the spiritual contortions of Pierre Menard, who in modern Paris was driven to express himself in Spanish, and in antique Spanish, and in locutions whose every contortion bears a strained and oblique relation to any values with which we are familiar. And it is doubtful whether we are in the presence of a work of art, if we cannot imagine what a man went through to produce it. But this fiction of Borges presents a hypothetical extreme case, uninhabitable like the summit of Everest. Like the summit of Everest it can serve as a vantage point.

From that vantage point look back over the decades after Defoe, and behold an entire civilization preoccupied with contortions like those of Pierre Menard, who counterfeited from *Don Quixote*. It is not only the time of Ireland's *Vortigern*, Chatterton's *Rowley,* and Mac-Pherson's *Ossian*, three borderline cases, but of outright and cheeky fraud on the one wing and of an esthetic of imitation on the other. Fake antiques were being manufactured wholesale in Rome for sale to travelers as Greek and Roman artifacts;[13] a famous picture shows, hanging

13. See R. H. Wilenski, *The Meaning of Modern Sculpture*, II.9.vii.f. See especially paragraphs 28 and 30, which suggest that the Venus de Milo and the Nike of Samothrace contain so much modern workmanship as to be classifiable as counterfeits.

in their frames, dozens of other famous pictures, the very details of their brushwork microscopically imitated; epics and mock-epics imitate the *Aeneid* and one another; pastorals imitate the *Eclogues* and Satires imitate Horace; Pope transposes to a new language Homer and Donne; everyone subsequently transposes Pope; and George after George, the unlucky Second (surnamed Augustus) still more than the First, who enjoyed cutting paper, was transmuted by not always ironic alchemy into the Emperor Augustus, who himself had transmuted himself into a god.

It was in the course of transmuting the second George into Augustus that Pope made his principal contribution to the theory of counterfeiting, so stunning an insight that he was to spend much of the seven years that remained to him recasting the *Dunciad* by its light. He discovered Pop Art.

He was busy at what Dr. Johnson surmised to have been his favorite amusement, imitating Horace; his text was the first epistle of the second book; and we may imagine his attention caught by the last eleven lines.

> Sedulitas autem stulte, quem diligit, urget . . .

Folly, however zealous, remains offensive, and whatever his singleness of motive there is no honor in being praised by an incompetent poet—

> Nec prave factis decorari versibus opto:

and what would an incompetent poet's praise of George Augustus look like? Might he not imitate this very Epistle ("To Augustus"), and invoke the ancient compliments to the King's serenity, the King's power of effecting wonders by inclining his head, and meanwhile (and justly) despair of his own adequacy to an Imperial theme:

Oh!

(what syllable better to launch a generous rhapsody?)

> Oh! could I mount on the Maeonian wing,
> Your Arms, your Actions, your Repose to sing!
> What seas you travers'd! and what fields you fought!
> Your Country's Peace, how oft, how dearly bought!
> How barb'rous rage subsided at your word,
> And Nations wonder'd while they dropp'd the sword!
> How, when you nodded, o'er the land and deep,
> Peace stole her wing, and wrapt the world in sleep . . .

And by a very tiny miscalculation—which generous heat surely excuses—might such a bard not overlook some connotations of "dearly," or place the royal Repose within memory's reach of the word "sleep," and set between them (most unfortunately) the word "nodded"? All these expressions are contained in L; to appraise their interactions we need to know whether the subfield is L_d, a dunce, or L_s, a satirist. The kingly repose, the imperious kingly nod, these by the alchemy of "sleep" become ridiculous if the poem is signed "A. Pope." If it is signed, say, "Ambrose Philips," or not signed, these trifling flaws become bubbles in a torrent of adulation. Pope's signature does not merely accept responsibility for the libel, it creates the libel: so delicate are the forces that govern the esthetics of fraud. Indeed not everyone saw the libel created; a writer in *Common Sense* (October 8, 1737), supposing Mr. Pope to be a poet "who but seldom meddles with publick Matters," singled out the Epistle as the only thing written on the government's side these last seven years.[14]

14. J. Butt, ed. *Pope: Imitations of Horace*, N. Y., 1946, xxxviii.

In the winter of 1742 Pope was rewriting *The Dunciad* as if a dunce had written it. *The Dunciad* (1728) had commenced in the mock-heroic way that Dryden sponsored:

> Books and the Man I sing, the first who brings
> The Smithfield Muses to the Ear of Kings.

Libros virumque: books and the man: a routine substitution of a word in Vergil's opening: though he had been sufficiently sophisticated in 1728 to imitate a nonexistent original, Homer's *Margites*. But now, dropping "Books and the Man," he addressed himself to the Pop *Dunciad,* imagining how a drudge infatuated with Milton would attempt the epic opening:

> The Mighty Mother, and her Son who brings
> The Smithfield Muses to the ear of Kings,
> I sing.

This bard stumbles into his kettledrums and falls headlong. A hideous cacophony (brings-Kings-sings); a failure to assess the compatability of end-stopped rhymes with a system based on caesurae; an insufficient breath, which terminates the opening period in mid-gesture: these Pope has imitated with the care a Lichtenstein bestows on comic-book panels, or a Warhol on soup labels. Yet thirty years earlier a small mock-epic had opened,

> What dire offence from amorous causes springs,
> What mighty contests rise from trivial things,
> I sing—

It is as though the blundering bard of *The Dunciad* had essayed the high wire from which Alexander Pope never slipped when he wrote *The Rape of the Lock*. For as man who was made to walk the ground can walk on a wire, so no one can formulate rules for the management of language that another cannot violate if he understands how; and understanding this, Pope in *The Dunciad,* imitating the catastrophic efforts of a dunce to imitate the epic manner by imitating an earlier Pope's imitation, supplies as intricate an example as we are ever likely to need of the esthetics of simulation.

Our century's more modest ventures in simulation rarely aspire beyond the Pope of the *Epistle to Augustus,* imitating not people trying to be Milton but people trying to be competent (as Charles Ives scored the vagaries of a village choir) or people trying to be unobtrusive (as Warhol reproduced the look of Brillo boxes). In such a process odd transvaluations occur; by way of self-effacement Ives and Warhol arrive at spectacle, and Hindemith, who aimed with his *musique d'ameublement* directly at inconspicuousness, lived to hear his pieces carefully listened to (like John Cage's silence) in concert. Consider, similarly, *le douanier* Rousseau; can we say he was trying to paint some other kind of picture and not succeeding? If so, what kind of picture? So we decide that he advanced, and meant to advance, the frontiers of painting. Was that what an American Primitive meant?

We mean, in the presence of a Primitive painting, something other than its painter meant; when we call Rousseau a greater painter than the anonymous frontier artisan, we mean presumably that we divine a smaller gap between our intentions and his own. The Primitive canvas, like a cigar-store Indian or a flowered chamber pot, is a cultural souvenir, beached by gone waves. It can of course itself be counterfeited, and the counterfeit, once detected, is a cultural allusion, much as the line "Those are pearls that were his eyes" in *The Waste Land* is transformed by our memory (or by Eliot's note) into an allusion. Such counterfeits, as in Robert Indiana's evocations of reaping machines and the stencilled letters on barns, exude a cushioning tranquillity, different in kind from the taxidermal tranquillity of *trompe l'oeil*. They are tranquil because we know what has replaced the things they simulate, and know that part of its meaning is the *effort* it has expended in replacing them. All along the frontier of obsolescence there is struggle; but the veritably obsolescent has retired. Hence it is tranquil; hence our illusion that its times were tranquil. And how will time deal with a Warhol soup-label or Brillo box? They assault us today with their stridency; it is an effort to look at them, like the effort of listening to an explosion. It may be that we can only bear to look at what we are no longer conscious of needing, and that our deepest fear is of contemplating our own needs.

That was the chief fear of the fears Swift exploited. Many things have been said about Augustan civilization. We can say one thing more, that related as it was to a philosophy which detached appearances from realities, a science which was learning to read the gone Past by looking at mute present objects (as Edward Gibbon looked at the ruins of Rome), and a cultivated class preoccupied with knowing simulacra of the prestigious, it was engaged as men were never to be again with massive experimentation on the relation of fear to fraud. Perhaps its principal masterpiece is a forged travel book complete with forged maps, introduced by a cousin of the nonexistent author who discusses the principles upon which he deleted from the manuscript thousands of words that were never written; we learn from it what horses talk about, and how men make shift to counterfeit horsey virtues, and are frightened by its genial implication that our world is more excremental than a horse's. The man who conceived it earned the undying gratitude of his countrymen for exposing, under an assumed name and in an assumed character, a scheme for flooding Ireland with counterfeit halfpence, and in his will he endowed a mental hospital. We cannot wonder that eventually the cult of sincerity had to be invented, to give us breathing space before Andy Warhol.

But our breathing-time has passed, and now the whole topic is back, its relevance reinforced by our immense proficiency at reproducing things, and by our simultaneous doubts about the value and meaning of personal identity. Accustomed as we are to the form letter, the mechanically reproduced signature, the edited Congressional Record, the doctored tape recording, the Xerox copy, the color photograph, the Van Gogh sunflowers in reproduction with the very texture of the canvas simulated, the documentary film with every scene carefully staged, and the millions upon millions of identical soup tins out of which we nourish bodies containing glass eyes and gold teeth; deriving our mathematics from the nonexistent Bourbaki and our culinary norms from the nonexistent Miss Crocker, devoted to comic strips drawn by substitutes and signed with dead men's names, avid, on our screens, not for drama imitating by rhythm and rhetoric but for detailed photographic records of events that never happened, events continuous with what the newspapers call reality, presided over by a chief executive with a suite full of ghosts: in such straits we are fascinated by synthetic spontaneity and by the subtleties of things that are not quite themselves. Joyce perfected a prose meant to look as though no one had composed it, a prose seemingly the exhalation of its subject, behind which the artist should disappear, "aloof, indifferent, paring his fingernails." (And what, we vainly ask, is the tone of the synthetic *Portrait*? Aloof? Idyllic? Sentimental? Satiric? As who should ask, what subsystem governs this specialization of system L? Is it L_1 or L_2 or L_3? Or none of these?) This prose of his lays upon the page glimpses of things and persons actually seen, snatches of conversations actually heard (hence the fallacy that the key to Joyce's work is somewhere in his life); for "he is a very bold man who dares to alter in the presentment . . . whatever he has seen and heard."[15] From this there follows his image of artist as priest, changing nothing of his materials except their use. And this invisible artist presiding over a mystery, for all his trappings of *fin-de-siècle* romance, seems closely related to Pope and Swift, who also pretended not to exist.

Joyce forged an autobiography and then imitated Homer; Eliot imitated Elizabethan drama; Pound put together a synthetic Latin classic. All three, simultaneously, affected to be imitating the mere surface confusion of their time's public and social life. In their lives they played rôles: the bourgeois father, the banker, the American bohemian in Europe. That Yeats elaborated the theory of the mask, that Pound's third and twenty-seventh published volumes

15. Joyce to Grant Richards, quoted in Herbert Gorman, *James Joyce*, V-iv.

are both called *Personae,* that the eighteen sections of *Ulysses* are written in eighteen different styles as though to acknowledge theories of a multiple Homer, that a note to *The Waste Land* invites us to find all its personages melting into one, and that the poem is packaged like the official poetry of a time when poetry is dead, with numbered lines and footnotes: these will no doubt seem to the eye of the future details as endemic to our age as the rites of forgery and masques of identity that strike our attention in the literature of the Augustans.

If we are to learn to see our time with the eye of the future, we shall have to recognize the strategies of the counterfeiter for what they are, understanding that he imitates not things but occasions, and that a work's historical context, real or feigned, is part of its meaning. To pretend, so many decades after Defoe, that the artist is best considered as a craftsman, and the work of art as mute as a Windsor chair, yielding up nothing but empirical information, is to ignore the lesson of generations of counterfeiters who restored the personal to a blank universe by seeming to suppress the person. For he returns, L_1, L_2, . . . L_n. The soup can that became an utterance might have been contrived to refute this fashionable hypothesis, so comforting to critics and so frigid for artists. What the artist's mere signature does is transform the soup can into a sort of word, totally inexplicit, totally assertive, inexplicably permanent. A word comes from a person, who intends it. A soup can is a soup can, in a different and less accessible universe.

IV

The Gulliver Game

. . . In a different and less accessible universe: the one in which Buster Keaton is normally trapped: a silent nightmare where hospital beds are blown by great winds through stables, past indifferent beasts, or footloose cows wander in Turkish baths, or, in a ship's galley scaled for feeding hundreds, two people, as though dreaming, must boil their two eggs in a gigantic cauldron, and contrive a Goldbergian opener, culminating in a mechanized hacksaw, to deal with obdurate cans.[1] The cauldrons and the cans inhabit this quiet world: it is theirs by right. Out of its vectors, as though by plunging his arm through a metaphysical curtain, Andy Warhol has purloined numerous soup tins, but there is no rescue for Keatonian Man.

Hour after hour, at sixteen glimpses per second, his plight is enacted with metronomic precision before crowds unaware that they themselves are sitting in total darkness twenty-seven minutes out of each sixty. At intervals they disperse, to resume their dialogue with their own machines: cars, locks, faucets, egg-beaters. The terms of this

1. Details from *Steamboat Bill Jr.* (1927), *Go West* (1925) and *The Navigator* (1924).

Mr. Alan Turing with Respirator and Chronometer
on His Way to a Mathematical Congress

dialogue constitute the greater part of their learning. Their children can open boxes before they can speak, or tie shoes before framing sentences, and will grow up, each of them, to own a car: which (William Faulkner wrote) he will lend to no one, "letting no other hand ever know the last secret forever chaste forever wanton intimacy of its pedals and levers."[2] If he acquires a human bride he will comfort her with machines when she chances to be sick of love.

These people (ourselves) spend their lives shaping and displacing matter: moving bits of it about according to the marks on them, tampering with the economy of its queer numb universe, melting it, pounding it, pigmenting it, hurling it at the moon. In every bedroom a half-minute's twiddling of thumb and forefinger is nightly stored by a spring, to be paid out again accurately all day long by trains of brass gears (fabricated among the Alps), that all other arrangements may be synchronized: because two pieces of matter, for instance two streetcars, cannot occupy the same space at the same time. Attention is riveted by processes, by any process for enhancing the symmetry of large or little objects. How are "twenty thousand needles thrown promiscuously into a box" to be arranged for sale with their points all facing one way? This problem once engaged many imaginations; by 1832 a solution had been devised which required only a child and a bit of cloth.

> The child puts on the forefinger of its right hand a small cloth cap or finger-stall, and rolling out of the heap from six to twelve needles, he keeps them down by the forefinger of the left hand, whilst he presses the forefinger of the right hand gently against their

2. William Faulkner, *Intruder in the Dust*, xi.

ends; those which have the points towards the right hand stick into the finger-stall; and the child, removing the finger of the left hand, slightly raises the needles sticking into the cloth, and then pushes them towards the left side. Those needles which had their eyes on the right hand do not stick into the finger cover, and are pushed to the heap on the right side previously to the repetition of this process. By means of this simple contrivance each movement of the finger, from one side to the other, carries five or six needles to their proper heap; whereas, in the former method, frequently only one was moved, and rarely more than two or three were transported at one movement to their place.[3]

This voice belongs to the Laureate of Process, Charles Babbage (1792-1871), as fascinating an intelligence as the age of Dickens and D'Israeli can show. His best prose is unmatched save by Swift's: a writer impassioned by the interactions of *things* will give us far better than a Carlyle or an Emerson (for whom things impede opinions) so many things, almost in an equal number of words. His minute curiosity supplies copious nouns, his devotion to process abundant verbs to link them. There are no gaps in his exposition because none in his understanding, when both are intent on a process all of whose steps are necessary and sufficient. Under Babbage's eye, for instance, a counterfeit broccoli-leaf takes form with enviable elegance:

A very beautiful mode of representing small branches of the most delicate vegetable productions in bronze has been employed by Mr. Chantrey. A

3. Charles Babbage, *Economy of Manufactures and Machinery*, London, 1832, sec. 11.

small strip of a fir-tree, a branch of holly, a curled leaf of broccoli, or any other vegetable production, is suspended by one end in a small cylinder of paper which is placed for support within a similarly formed tin case: the finest river silt, carefully separated from all the coarser particles, and mixed with water so as to have the consistency of cream, is poured into the paper cylinder by small portions at a time, carefully shaking the plant a little after each addition, in order that its leaves may be covered, and that no bubbles of air may be left. The plant and its mould are now allowed to dry, and the yielding nature of the paper allows the loamy coating to shrink from the outside. When this is dry it is surrounded by a coarser substance; and, finally, we have the twig with all its leaves embedded in a perfect mould. This mould is carefully dried, and then gradually heated to a red heat. At the ends of some of the leaves or shoots, wires have been left to afford air-holes by their removal, and in this state of strong ignition a stream of air is directed into the hole formed by the end of the branch. The consequence is, that the wood and leaves which had been turned into charcoal by the fire, are now converted into carbonic acid by the current of air; and after some time the whole of the solid matter of which the plant consisted is completely removed, leaving a hollow mould, bearing on its interior all the minutest traces of its late vegetable occupant. When this process is completed, the mould being still kept at nearly a red heat, receives the fluid metal, which by its weight, either drives the very small quantity of air, which at that high temperature remains behind, out through the air-holes, or compresses it into the pores of the very porous substance of which the mould is formed.[4]

4. Babbage, *Economy*, sec. 79.

This is excerpted from a sequence of thirty-five pages, where under eight headings some sixty-one methods are detailed for making an object that shall be exactly like another object: a counterfeiter's very *vade mecum*. The sensibility of a Marianne Moore was formed on a connoisseurship of like precisions. And it was written while Tennyson was being satisfied to arrange words into such configurations as "pensive thought and aspect pale," and to rhyme "the murmur of the strife" with "the toil of life."[5] Babbage was to take notice of his young contemporary's dealings with the language a decade later, when

> Every minute dies a man
> Every minute one is born

drew from him the remark that the world's population was in fact constantly increasing: "I would therefore take the liberty of suggesting that in the next edition of your excellent poem the erroneous calculation to which I refer should be corrected as follows: 'Every moment dies a man/And one and a sixteenth is born'." This figure, he added, was a concession to metre, since the actual ratio was 1 : 1.167. Tennyson did eventually blur his assertion to the extent of changing "minute" to "moment."[6]

Babbage's mastery of expository prose reflects his unique mastery of the sort of world toward which, since the Royal Society was founded, expository prose had been striving to adequate itself. He was the father of the digital computer: not simply its projector, but the designer, in rigorous detail, of mechanisms so near the frontiers of the

5. Tennyson, "Margaret," 1833.
6. P. and E. Morrison, eds., *Charles Babbage and his Calculating Engines*, N. Y., 1961, xxiii. A slightly different version is given by B. V. Bowden, *Faster than Thought*, London, 1953, 332.

gear-and-lever technology for which he conceived them that his contemporaries forgot them as chimerical and left his successors, in the vacuum-tube age, to work out their first principles all over again.

He was also the father of Operations Analysis, applying its methods, in engagingly discursive fashion, to the Post Office, to pin-making, to the entire Industrial economy. Pin-making, in seven parts (drawing, straightening, pointing, twisting, heading, tinning, papering) he details according to the majestic principles of the Division of Labor, computing the wages expended on each pin, per stage, in millionths of a penny. We learn that four men, four women and two children devote to a pound of product (5,546 pins) an aggregate of just 7.6892 hours, a man who twists and cuts heads being paid 14.3 times as much per day (or per pin) as the boy who assists him, and the man who draws wire just over twice as much as the woman who, with the aid of a comb and a jig, arranges the finished pins in paper packets.[7] So the factory; so the society; so the economy; so the management of a single philosopher's day; and Babbage, habitually attentive to the appropriate allocation of effort, arranged that while busy observing the flanks of Mount Vesuvius he should be at the same time carried bodily up it; and this, according to the steepness of the slope, by horses, mules, or men in turn.

Processes divided are ripe for mechanization, since if we divide them sufficiently far we arrive at the classic Simple Machines; Babbage accordingly details the workings of a pin-making machine lately invented in America.[8] Intellectual processes are similarly divisible, and at last simi-

7. Babbage, *Economy*, sec. 170-178.
8. Babbage, *Economy*, sec. 181-182.

larly susceptible of mechanical imitation; hence the great dream of the Analytical Engine, which haunted the second half of Babbage's life, and of which the finished detail drawings alone cover a thousand square feet. This was to embody the whole science of operations, an operation being defined as "any process which alters the mutual relation of two or more things."[9] Its Mill, where the operations were conducted, was to draw data from a Store, where intermediate results were available, and then deposit other data in that Store. Babbage thought of his machine as a factory, not a brain; it was for his twentieth century successors to speak of a Memory. His most informed apologist, Lord Byron's daughter, observed that the Analytical Engine *"weaves algebraic patterns,* just as the Jacquard loom weaves flowers and leaves."[10] The analogy with the Jacquard loom is just, for the Engine (prompted by the loom) was to receive its data on punched cards (punched cards!) and on punched cards likewise acquire the instructions (we say "program") according to which it would assume the sequence of configurations appropriate to the problem in hand. Babbage, it is clear, had conceived in 1834 the IBM card, perhaps not quite foreseeing, despite the paradigms in his *Economy of Manufactures,* a world fretting over being punched, folded, stapled or mutilated. He also invented, decades before the typewriter, means by which the Engine should print out its result, to save the proofing errors consequent on a human typesetter; and as for the human attendant, who would be summoned by a bell from time to time to make good certain gaps in the

9. Morrison & Morrison, *Babbage,* 247.
10. Morrison & Morrison, *Babbage,* 252.

Store, he would insert the card for which the Engine called, and wait for it to verify that he had indeed inserted the right card, and if he had not "it would have discovered the mistake, and have rung a louder bell to call the attention of its guide, who on looking at the proper place, would see a plate above the logarithm he had just put in with the word *'wrong'* engraven upon it."[11]

This transfigured alarm clock would have weighed several tons, and been ten or twelve feet long, all brass and steel and pewter, driven by springs and weights, and been capable of any computation whatever, even of playing chess or composing music; and it nearly broke Babbage's heart. No one, certainly not the British government, would put up a penny towards its construction. Near the end of his life he was still refining the drawings, and devising yet simpler effectors for its numerous functions. He was aware that as soon as it existed it would "necessarily guide"—as have ENIAC, MANIAC and their successors—"the future course of the science." At seventy-two he set down with ripe lucidity the gist of its working:

> Thus it appears that the whole of the conditions which enable a *finite* machine to make calculations of *unlimited* extent are fulfilled in the Analytical Engine. The means I have adopted are uniform. I have converted the infinity of space, which was required by the conditions of the problem, into the infinity of time. The means I have employed are in daily use in the art of weaving patterns. It is accomplished by systems of cards punched with various holes strung together to any extent which may be demanded. Two large boxes, the one empty and the

11. Morrison & Morrison, *Babbage*, 329.

other filled with perforated cards, are placed before and behind a polygonal prism, which revolves at intervals upon its axis, and advances through a short space, after which it immediately returns.

A card passes over the prism just before each stroke of the shuttle; the cards that have passed hang down until they reach the empty box placed to receive them, into which they arrange themselves one over the other. When the box is full, another empty box is placed to receive the coming cards, and a new full box on the opposite side replaces the one just emptied. As the suspended cards on the entering side are exactly equal to those on the side at which the others are delivered, they are perfectly balanced, so that whether the formulae to be computed be excessively complicated or very simple, the force to be exerted always remains nearly the same.[12]

That is Babbage's beatific vision, that slow settling of suspended cards into a receiving box for ever. There is perhaps no parallel for so detailed and dogged a creation in a technology verging on obsolescence, unless the creation of the brontosaurus, which half swam and half walked, and thrilled throughout its slow ganglia, and metabolized plants, and was awesome.

Its awesome creator was once heard to doubt whether he had ever spent a happy day in his life. Like an Ur-Keaton, Babbage frequently seems marooned in the wrong universe. He and Disraeli, for example, existed in compliance with different logics, like an eye and a cinder; and yet they co-existed; Disraeli as Chancellor of the Exchequer gave the Engine its *coup de grâce* in 1852. The right uni-

12. Babbage, *Passages from the Life of a Philosopher*, 128-9; reprinted in Morrison and Morrison, 63.

The Bards of Twickenham and of Chios Strike Their Lyres

verse would have been free of bandits, parliamentarians, organ-grinders, and so managed as to leave a philosopher in peace. Disencumbered of the little precautions he took, when travelling, against the possibility of being held for ransom; delivered from wrangles with the kind of public man who wondered whether, if the wrong figures were put into the Engine, the right answers might still come out, and yet had influence on the Engine-making funds; free to use fruitfully that substantial part of his working-power (twenty-five per cent, as he computed) which street musicians annihilated when they shattered trains of thought, he might have tinkered happily for a lifetime at useful problems: generating tables of numbers by machinery, expressing by signs any machinery's action, tabulating the pulse and respiration rate of Mammalia (for the collection of which facts, he noted, "the pig fair at Pavia and the book fair at Leipsic equally placed before me menageries"), enumerating, to the inexpressible benefit of actuaries, the relative frequency of occurrence of the causes of breaking plate glass windows, ascertaining the effect of the cost of verification (we say, quality control) on the cost of any article, preparing dictionaries for the use of cipher-breakers, composing a monograph (unpublished) "On the Art of Opening all Locks," together with a plan of partially defeating the method.[13]

> But I was thinking of a plan
> To dye my whiskers green,

said the White Knight,

13. Gleaned from *Passages from the Life of a Philosopher*. The "List of Mr. Babbage's Printed Papers" at the end of that book is reprinted in Morrison and Morrison, 372-377.

> And always use so large a fan
> That they could not be seen.

And did Conan Doyle know of Babbage? He was fit to be Holmes's mentor.

The right and wrong universes were partially coincident. All these things and more he did do, or partly do, amid harrassments; and he rode about Europe in a coach of his own devising, in which he could sleep at full length, boil an egg, pack away (without folding) plans, drawings and dress-coats, and stow in appropriate pockets various currencies, travelling books, telescopes "and many other conveniences," these latter including such portable curiosities as might earn rapport with savants, artisans and monarchs abroad: notably a dozen gold buttons, irridescent because ruled with diffraction gratings, and a compact stomach pump "in great request from its novelty and utility. I had many applications for permission to make drawings of it, to which I always most willingly acceded."[14] Even when annoyances do not obtrude, the Man of Sense, circa 1840, has become Buster Keaton in apotheosis, engaged in his choreographic dialogue with mute permutable matter; and the more they obtrude, as into his fallen world obtrude they must, the more Keatonian he. Consider, as a potential shooting script, the heads of Babbage's treatise on organ grinders and other street nuisances:

> Various classes injured—Instruments of Torture—
> Encouragers; Servants, Beer-shops, Children, Ladies
> of elastic virtue—Effects on the Musical Profession
> —Retaliation—Police themselves disturbed—In-
> valids distracted—Horses run away—Children run

14. Babbage, *Passages*, 373.

over—A Cab-stand placed in the Author's street attracts Organs—Mobs shouting out his Name—Threats to Burn his House—Disturbed in the middle of the night when very ill—An average number of Persons are always ill—Hence always disturbed—Abusive Placards—Great Difficulty of getting Convictions—Got a Case for the Queen's Bench—Found it useless—A Dead Sell—Another Illustration—Musicians give False Name and Address—Get Warrant for Apprehension—They keep out of the way—Offenders not yet found and arrested by the Police—Legitimate Use of Highways—An Old Lawyer's Letter to *The Times*—Proposed Remedies; Forbid entirely—Authorize Police to seize the Instrument and take it to the Station—An Association for Prevention of Street Music proposed.[15]

Visualize the Philosopher in quest of a policeman, followed by a crowd of young children and shouting vagabonds. "When I turn round and survey my illustrious tail, it stops; if I move towards it, it recedes: the elder branches are then quiet—sometimes they even retire, wishing perhaps to avoid my future recognition. The instant I turn, the shouting and the abuse are resumed, and the mob again follow at a respectful distance." Or consider the contortions of sub-plot when, his susceptibility growing notorious, neighbors commenced "purchasing worn-out or damaged wind-instruments, which they are incapable of playing, but on which they produced a discordant noise for the purpose of annoying me." And weigh, in the eye of this hurricane, his insouciance when one neighbor, a workman, opened his window day after day at noon-time

15. Babbage, *Passages*, 337. Morrison and Morrison reprint his analytical chapter-headings complete, 385-391.

and leaning out of it blew a penny tin whistle in the direction of Babbage's garden for half an hour: "I simply noted the fact in a memorandum-book, and then employed the time he thought he was destroying, in taking my daily exercise, or in any other outdoor mission my pursuits required. After a perseverance in this course during many months, he discontinued the annoyance, but for what reason I never knew." Keaton dealing with a cow was never finer. *Magna est ordinatio et praevalebit.*

Out of human fury and mire the familiar eccentric scientist has taken form, Aristotle of dark Satanic mills where children align the eyes of ten thousand needles from dawn to dark, and men give thought to means of counterfeiting in thousands the elegancies hands once shaped. (John Ruskin's rage is mounting throughout the century.) As the beggars of Ireland affronted the Modest Proposer, so do men hinder the Philosopher. Things console him, things in their myriad combinations. Intent on his great brass brain, meant to permute and distinguish and associate according to laws whatever comes into it (John Locke mimed in hardware), he behaves ever more sensibly, ever more madly, while about him storms of organ grinders swirl: the last protests of what would be a lost, human world had the protestors the insight to do more than hoot against genius. When a century later the organ grinders have retired, genius is still eccentric, though less hooted at, amid our orderly greyness. Like the universe of atomized fact to which it corresponds, the species is stable. Though he rides no longer in a custom-fitted coach, a wizard of electronic computation, circa 1940, is still as indomitably rational as Babbage. Thus:

Mr. W. B. Yeats' Aspiration toward Mechanical Birdhood Collides
with the Present State of Vaucanson's Duck

Alan M. Turing (1912-1954) wore a gas mask in the neighborhood of wartime Bletchley while riding his bicycle. He did this to coddle his hayfever. He is known to have tied an alarm clock around his middle in lieu of a forgotten wristwatch. When the bicycle manifested an insecure chain he dealt with it as man to man, not assaulting its nonconformity but tactfully recording symptoms. The chain came off after x revolutions of the pedal; by counting these revolutions he could have a restraining heel ready, and the tedium of counting was later relieved by a mechanical counting device. Further analysis disclosed a relationship embracing three numbers, which denominated respectively turns of the pedal, links in the chain, and spokes in the rear wheel: this relationship in turn directed attention to a certain damaged link which passed at long but fixed intervals a certain bent spoke. The spoke was straightened. "This done," his biographer (and mother) affirms, "there was no more need to bring a bottle of turpentine and piece of rag to the office to clean his hands after replacing the chain whenever it did come off."[16] She adds that a bicycle mechanic would have fixed it in five minutes.

The man in the gas mask resembled an automaton; the crotchety bicycle could not have been more circumspectly treated had it been a person. The relationship between persons and the automata that counterfeit them has never been more suggestively explored than by Turing, who invented in the process the Turing Machine, which has never been built, and Turing's Game, which has never been played.

The Turing Machine is the ultimate computer, which

16. Sara Turing, *Alan M. Turing*, Cambridge, 1959, 69.

suitably programmed can simulate any lesser machine: a machine for computing square roots, for example, or assigning mates, or translating Russian. Each such machine is a "state" Z_1 of the Turing Machine Z. Set up the Turing Machine for any of these tasks, and it will be impossible to guess that it was not designed for that task alone. It is the aptest of counterfeiters; it can even simulate to perfection a machine twice as large and complicated as it is, which is as though the village idiot, suitably methodized, could simulate Shakespeare (albeit slowly). To effect this (and to write *Hamlet?*) it needs nothing more than the ability to scrutinize inch by inch an indefinitely long paper tape; keep track of its place in a table of designated responses; respond according as it sees a mark or no mark; in response move the tape inch by inch in either direction; and/or write a mark; and/or erase a mark. That is all. That is Shakespeare (implicitly: Turing didn't say so). For the tape, written and erased, is a life's experience: what more had Donne, or Dante, or Herman Wouk? Do not say, his learning; he had experienced his learning. "A thought to Donne," wrote T. S. Eliot, "was an experience; it modified his sensibility." It marked, erased, moved his tape. That tape is the machine's whole outside world. There are some things written on it before the action starts. They are the machine's environment. There is a "program" (its heredity and innate reflexes). The rest is learning.[17]

17. This idealized machine was first described by Turing in a 1937 paper, "On Computable Numbers . . .", reprinted in M. Davis, ed., *The Undecidable*, Hewlett, N. Y., 1965. John von Neumann's exposition, reprinted in J. R. Newman, *The World of Mathematics*, N. Y., 1956, vol. IV, 2093-4, incorporates some helpful simplifications. See also M. Davis, *Computability & Unsolvability*, N. Y., 1958, ch. 1. Irving Adler's *Thinking Machines*, N. Y., 1961, chapter 3, offers Turing "programs" with which the reader may experiment for himself.

This machine is in fact the Babbage Engine, as Turing himself says, though abstracted away to a shadow. Fiddling with its tape, it will be excruciatingly slow, but parallel systems of similar design will speed it up, and electrifying a large number of such parallel systems will give us the modern digital computer. By deriving the design in this way we learn that our multi-transistored toy is essentially a simulator.

And *Hamlet* may be the inevitable outcome of certain accumulated experiences reacting within a certain genetic makeup; and if this is true (a large "if," which we shall be querying) then a machine in the proper state, properly prodded with stimuli, will write *Hamlet*, and that state of the Turing Machine can be said to simulate Shakespeare.

From which follows the Turing Game: for a man may be a special state of the Turing Machine, one of its special states, if we only knew how to write the program. Can we perhaps program it so that it will pass, if not as *this* man, as some man? Turing confronted this possibility in 1950. Attacking the tedious question whether machines can think (a question which never occurred to Babbage) he proposed a game for three players. It differs from most games in that each of them is trying to do something different. One player is a machine; it is trying to pass itself off as a person. Another is a person, trying to make it clear that he *is* a person. The third is an observer, trying to decide which is which. All communication is by electric teletypewriter, with the observer in a separate room.[18]

18. Turing, "Thought and Machine Processes," in Newman, *World of Mathematics,* 2099-2123. Such simulations have since received, notably from Professor Donald Mackay, much more sophisticated attention than Turing gave them, but for our purposes his proposed game suffices.

Can he hope to distinguish an electric brain from a human one by observing the answers it types? We can arrange for the machine to make occasional typing errors, to improve the camouflage; and if it is asked mathematical questions a delaying mechanism can keep it from delivering the product of two eight-digit numbers in a few microseconds. It could even give such products wrongly from time to time, and remark that it was weak at arithmetic as far back as the second grade.

We shall have to equip it with answers to such questions as "What was the name of your second-grade teacher?" In fact we shall have to equip it with a citizenship, a confirmation sponsor, an opinion on whether its maker exists, a preference among salad dressings, an entire life history. This is a taxing but not unfamiliar problem, comparable to providing a secret agent with a new identity and a cover story (our light fiction is obsessed with problems of counterfeiting). When the spy of fiction encounters a crisis for which his mentors had not thought to prepare him, and must proceed on his own, the usual moral of the story has him not essentially someone's agent but a man, or a better agent for being also a man, but this moral is intended to flatter the reader of the story, who is generally human— if spy stories were written for the entertainment of machines they would be quite different.

Clearly Turing's Game would be over if the questioner happened to probe a negligence on the part of the programmer, much as in 1944 a German infiltrator was captured because no one had told him how the cellophane comes off American cigarette packages, and some of his confederates because they could not name Tarzan's mate or Superman's alter ego.[19] These are problems of detail; Turing presupposes a machine that has received all the programming it needs. Could we find out, in that case, that we were dealing with a program rather than a person? The bishop is investigating something of that sort when he asks the catechism class to put answers "in their own words," and Turing suggests that the British custom of following up a written examination with a *viva* has similar aims. He even gives a sample of a dialogue intended to find out whether the candidate, William Shakespeare, really understands a sonnet he has written or has allowed poetic diction to spin at random, and indicates that such an interview, far from opening up glimpses into a soul, is a fencing-match not beyond the skill of a cunning programmer. What Shakespeare—or anyone—knows about himself is another question; and we have no way of guessing what a machine knows about itself.

As to the general question, whether you can find out if someone is human by talking to him, Turing's answer was no, ideally you cannot tell; and he committed himself to the prediction that by A.D. 2000 it would be possible to make computers play the game so well "that an average interrogator will not have more than a seventy percent chance of making the right identification after five minutes of questioning." This means that the technology our grandchildren will inherit will not cause them practical confusion between people and machines more than thirty percent of the time; Turing was perhaps not allowing for the possibility that people will grow more machine-like.

19. B. Ehrlich, *Resistance in France,* N. Y., Signet Books, 110.

Turing's question had been asked, at least in principle, long before 1950. One might say that the possibility of a pseudo-man first confronted the fourth-century skirmishers over the Sabellian heresy, which held that the human nature of Christ was illusory. The human nature of Christ is admittedly a special case, despite its dialectical and practical interest. It was the seventeenth century that raised the more general question of ascertaining the human nature of anybody. The empirical philosophers of that age adopted what is essentially Turing's strategy, situating themselves outside of a man to see what could be found out about him by observing his behavior, and Descartes speculated that so long as an automaton kept its mouth shut (for Descartes did not foresee programmed conversation) it could baffle a Turing observer.[20]

But consider what actually happens when you elect to examine the nature of man while situating yourself outside of that nature: you yourself elect not to be human. You decide that what you know about yourself is best neglected. You are going to be an observer of man, and a recorder of facts about man, but you are not going to be a man, for fear of corrupting your observations with what you know already. You are going to play Turing's game as if not only one of the beings observed, but also the observer, was a machine. This makes no difference to Turing's game at all, since the observer can derive no advantage from being human, and hence incur no disadvantage from being mechanical, so long as he is simply trying to tell a man and a machine apart. But it makes a great difference to the related project of learning some-

20. *Discourse on Method*, v; and see the references given by Noam Chomsky, *Cartesian Linguistics*, N. Y., 1966, note 9.

thing about what it is to be human. What you can tell about *that* by being a man, and what you can tell about it by observing a man, are simply incommensurable.

By Newton's time the planets had proved to trace elliptical orbits, not the circular ones we find congenial, and bodies to fall not in proportion to the tug they exercise on our muscles, but solely in proportion to the distance in feet from point of release to point of impact. The better to purify the observations by which such knowledge is gained, men learned to follow method, not caprice; to give all facts equal weight rather than stress the facts common sense finds important; to discipline the senses as though they were recording devices, and wherever possible to replace them by recording devices: the thermometer, the yardstick, the pendulum clock. We learned then to cherish the pure detachment which telescope and microscope confer on the eye, and to exercise a comparable detachment when we are using no telescope nor no microscope, but the very eye with which we regard the things we love. Such is the discipline of becoming, for specific purposes, something other than a human being.

This alarmingly tempting discipline frees its subscriber from worry about those Latin words ending in *-tas* at which we have already glanced: *equinitas, caninitas, humanitas.* He need not puzzle over the quality which constitutes horseness, he need only observe manifestations. The word *equinitas* alters; it is a Gothic parvenu, and very likely denotes nothing real. But the word *humanitas* alters also, and that alteration is more serious. For the word *humanitas* is not parvenu but classical, and before it took on its scholastic sense it had an older sense, harder to encapsulate. In the way that no horse can cease to be a horse, no man can cease to be a man; but the word *humanitas* from its earliest recorded uses seems to designate qualities which human beings do not always possess, and which some of them never possess, and others possess intermittently, and still others lose: a norm of behavior grounded in common feelings, and beyond that, the explicit cultivation and refinement of those feelings and that behavior, the end of that branch of studies which came to be called the humanities.

The Latin dictionary exhibits Cicero ringing change after change on this word, speaking of "communis humanitatis jus," the common law of humanity, or the duty "quod est humanitatis tuae," to which the very condition of being human prompts you. He defines it sometimes by pairing it with a second word: "pro sua clementia atque humanitate," his mildness and humanity, or "pro tua facilitate et humanitate," where "facilitas" means something like "good nature"; in one revealing passage he speaks of the possibility of the hearts of men, now brutalized by obsession with war, being recalled "ad humanitatem atque mansuetudinem," to humanity and clemency. If men can be recalled to *humanitas,* then *humanitas* is something men can forsake: forsake by forgetting.

For Cicero it is always something men can forsake: a human virtue, the specifically human virtue, but not the inseparable human essence. Horses cannot lose their *equinitas* because their being horses does not depend on their remembering to be horses, but men can lose *humanitas.* And to start losing it is easy, since beginning with our most harmonious feelings, it extends to our most appropriate mental possessions: the mental cultivation befitting a man. It denotes, said Erwin Panofsky, "the quality which distinguishes man not only from animals, but also, and even more so, from him who belongs to the species *homo* without deserving the name of *homo humanus*; from the vulgarian or barbarian who lacks *pietas* and *paideia*—that is, respect for moral values and that gracious blend of learning and urbanity which we can only circumscribe by the discredited word 'culture.' "[21] Thus Cicero castigates one whom he finds "sine ulla bona arte, sine humanitate, sine ingenio, sine litteris": uncouth, unlettered, inhumane.

As Cicero twines other words about *humanitas*—*comitas, facilitas, mansuetudo, clementia, doctrina, litterae, eruditio*—he seems to unfold and explicate the assumption that civilized people will already understand *humanitas* to subsume them all. To be fully human is to be all these things. And it is possible not to be fully human: possible, and fatally easy: easy when, like Turing's computer, you have been taught chains of answers out of a program, like the busy impostors castigated in *A Tale of a Tub* who have "become *Scholars* and *Wits,* without the Fatigue of *Reading* or of *Thinking*": indebted to *Indexes,* and *Systems and Abstracts;* to *Quotations* "plentifully gathered, and bookt in Alphabet"; to "judicious Collectors of *bright Parts,* and *Flowers,* and *Observanda's,*" and thus, in a few weeks, "capable of managing the profoundest, and most universal Subjects. For, what tho' his *Head* be empty, provided his *Common-place-Book* be full."[22] It is this man,

21. Erwin Panofsky, *Meaning in the Visual Arts*, Garden City, 1955, 2.
22. *A Tale of a Tub*, vii.

mutatis mutandis, that Turing says you cannot tell from a man. As Vaucanson's duck implies, while we do not see the mechanism, an egg and ducklinghood, so a Turing Machine, suitably instructed, implies the long flowering of *humanitas.* And the other impostor, *homo non humanus,* is the observer schooled to regard with disciplined niceness the present instant: the empiricist on whose "sublime and refined Point of Felicity" Swift memorably rounded, calling it "The Serene Peaceful State of being a Fool among Knaves:"[23] Lemuel Gulliver, for instance, who observes, observes, observes, and is one of the most insidiously sympathetic characters in fiction. For it is attractive to be relieved of the obligation to seem, in the traditional sense, civilized: not to have to undergo the long slow process of shaping one's taste and judgment, but only to invest one's formative years in "navigation, and other parts of the mathematics," and having to be sure read during one's leisure hours on shipboard "the best authors ancient and modern," to take refuge behind a clean face, a well-brushed coat, and the assertion, in every crux, that one has verified one's facts.

Generations of readers have been playing Turing's game with Gulliver since 1726 without being quite able to decide whether he is human or not, so thoroughly does he play the dehumanized observer. He is the Compleat Empiricist; he is Empiricism itself, trousered and shirted: Empiricism elevated into a life style, and rendered capable of a language that surprisingly resembles English. This language differs from English in a few trifling particulars.

23. *A Tale of a Tub*, ix. This book becomes much less puzzling once we realize how much of it is a counter-empirical tract.

It has little syntactic variety; subjects tend to come before verbs and objects after them, while qualifying phrases are linked to substantives with diagrammatic accuracy. It is nearly devoid of figuration; it seems unaware of the vast suggestive resources of English idiom; it will only assert, as though the natural operation of the mind were a sequence of assertions. And it abridges its labors with audible relief whenever it can incorporate an expression of number. In fact it will only explicate what it can not quantify; there are eight expressions of quantity in the first three sentences, which carry the author through all the seminal years of his life. Even courtship is quantified: "Being advised to alter my condition," writes Gulliver, "I married Mrs. Mary Burton, second daughter to Mr. Edmond Burton, hosier in Newgate Street, with whom I received four hundred pounds for a portion." "With whom I received" is delicious.

If we heard this in the course of Turing's Game, would we decide straightway that we were dealing with the machine? We might; and we might be ill-advised. We might equally well say that we are dealing with a man who lacks what the ancients called *pietas* ("dutiful conduct towards the gods, one's parents, one's family, one's benefactors, one's country"). Of *pietas* Gulliver displays only occasional rudiments. He does not mention God, of whom he seems not to have heard, not even when he tells us of the mercy to which he confided himself at the time of his first shipwreck: he confided himself, he says, "to the mercy of the waves." His family seldom sees him. His benefactors are chronicled and forgotten. No web of sentiment and obligation draws him tighter, as the years pass, into a system of human affection; we read very near the end how "as soon as I entered the house, my wife took me in her arms and kissed me, at which, not having been used to the touch of that odious animal for so many years, I fell in a swoon for almost an hour": no doubt checking his watch as he fell. An ancient would also find him lacking in *paideia*, that elusive incorporation into one's mind of the viable past, to draw near which is to incorporate that which we are. Of this process, so far as he has dabbled in it, Gulliver has two things to say: that he spent three years at Emmanuel College, Cambridge, and that while a young man at sea he read the best authors. Two sentences only are devoted to his dealings with that complex mental heritage which distinguishes *homo humanus* from the barbarian: and an account of no more than two sentences is adequate to the results, so far as we can judge them.

And we can judge a great deal; we are meant to judge a great deal; to judge Gulliver; to sharpen our mental apprehension on him. For Swift's great irony amounts to this, that whereas Gulliver fancies himself the accidental emissary of the human race to parts unknown, and hence the perpetual observer and recorder, it is Gulliver himself for the most part who is constantly under observation. Swift was the real inventor of Turing's game, the object of which is to see what we can tell about a man if we have reason to wonder whether he may be an artifact. The three positions in the game are occupied, respectively, by Gulliver; by ourselves, who are presumably human, partakers in *humanitas, homines humani*; and by various other creatures who may or may not be human, or quasi-human, but are as apt in empirical disciplines as Gulliver himself, and a good deal readier to spot an inconsistency. They observe him at least as closely as he them, and more than once he is put to the trouble of formally explaining human values to them, he who has so little notion of what it may mean to be human. This great chattering booby, this casually programmed talking machine, he is *our* spokesman, *our* ambassador, the player who must prove that he is human while a giant or a horse occupies the observer's seat. And yes, he is our representative; we have no right to complain, for he represents a modern ultimate, carrier and incarnation of the values we really value: notably accuracy, cleanliness, and the power to adjust. Compared with Swift's, Turing's formulation of the game seems almost trivial.

The Gulliver we can see is quite as peculiar as the Gulliver the beings in the book see. The most evident thing about him is surely his utter ignorance of everything save navigation, a little applied mathematics, and medicine (though as ship's physician he seems unashamed to report that the crews are perpetually sick). Civilization is memory; if we know more than our fathers, they are (in T. S. Eliot's phrase) that which we know. History, the classics, the works which we have learned to call humane letters, as indispensable to our cultural identity as are our private memories to our personal identity, all of these are as if unknown to him. It is surely no accident that his journey draws motif after motif from the *Odyssey,* which for all we can tell he has never read; nor that he spends nine pages on the Struldbrugs, who live forever, first rhapsodizing over the thought of an earthly immortality, then dismayed at a spectacle of eternal decreptitude, all the while unaware of the attention that has already been devoted to this theme: never having heard of the fate of the Sibyl of Cumae, or of the miseries of Tithonus. The Brobdingnagians never remind him of the Cyclops, nor the Houyhnhnms of the Centaurs, who were the wisest creatures in Greece. All that cycle of classical narrative which forms a moral terminology among civilized men has never existed for him. Our attention may be distracted from these lapses by their consonance with the style, which an empirical hygiene has purged of classical allusion on the ground that literary tricks impede the record of observation; to say as much is to say that we ourselves, unless the words remind us constantly of the classics, forget their relevance. We have made a long step toward our own dehumanization in putting them aside in a special place, to be tended by surly men called scholars and never to be touched except when the mood is, as it never seems to be, just right.

And Gulliver resembles ourselves in this too, that he has learned to regard history as a spectacle. He falls in with some sorcerers who have the power to summon up out of the past "whatever persons I would choose to name, and in whatever numbers among all the dead from the beginning of the world to the present time, and command them to answer any question I should think fit to ask." It is a philosopher's dream; and Gulliver dreams of entertainment. He desires to see Alexander the Great at the head of his army, and is entertained with this vision, on a wide screen and no doubt with stereophonic sound. And on being privileged to question Alexander the pupil of Aristotle, he asks him only this, whether it is true that he was poisoned. His next request is to see Hannibal crossing the Alps, elephants and all; and his question for Hannibal, when the star steps forward out of this spectacle, is a technological one: is it true that he employed vinegar to dissolve inconvenient rocks? Hannibal assures him that, no, he had no vinegar. Clearly Gulliver has an eye for minutiae: he has missed a brilliant career as a classical scholar. Clearly too, he has no notion at all of what the past has to teach. All is fact, corporeal fact; there are no moral facts, there is no drama, there is no *paideia*.

And that is the reason for his very poor showing when, in the second and fourth books, in the court of Brobdingnag and before the talking horses, he undertakes the Psalmist's challenge, "What is man?" If there is one being in the world who has no notion of the scope of that question, that being is Gulliver. He thinks that man is a rational animal. A computer is likewise a rational animal, most rational; and so are Swift's horses, animals—and rational too. There is really no point in Gulliver's competing with them, but compete he does.

We have our first sight of Turing's Game in the second book, when the learned men of Brobdingnag set themselves the problem, what is this creature that has come among them? We readers think we know that it is a man. But the Brobdingnagians know what a man is: a man is a being like themselves, seventy feet tall. And they are able to pick up this specimen, and examine it, and note its hominoid shape, and puzzle over the fact that it seems capable of learning their language; and they conclude that what they are dealing with is a *relplum scalcath*; very learned words of theirs, which may be interpreted into learned words of ours, *lusus naturae*; which words may be further interpreted, a flaw in the continuity of nature: something that has no business existing. It is amusing to reflect that a computer, since it works by natural laws, is not a flaw in the continuity of nature at all. *It* has a right to exist, in the same universe with the magnetic poles and the rotating earth, the cherry stones that remember how to make cherries and the glaciers that shear off the sides of mountains. It is ourselves who have no strictly natural business existing here. One can imagine the forces of natural evolution eventually producing a computer. It is harder to imagine them producing even Gulliver.

The learned men of Brobdingnag, when they decide that Gulliver has no business existing, are perhaps misled by his size. The King of Brobdingnag, however, plays the game under Turing conditions, attending to the other player's conversation, not his stature. And the more Gulliver talks to him, the more the King becomes convinced that if indeed Gulliver speaks for a race of beings like himself, then that race has no business existing; it is "the most pernicious race of little odious vermin that nature ever suffered to crawl upon the surface of the earth." This is Gulliver's fault, perhaps, since he talks so much about wars and plagues and poisons; he has been, we may be tempted to decide, badly programmed. If we think that, let us attend to how he fares among the horses.

For among the horses Turing's Game has assumed clearer contours. Gulliver comes among them a being quite different from themselves: he goes on two legs, he has no hooves. But he resembles rather closely a species with which they are already familiar, a species of beings that

Mr. Andy Warhol Fetches a Work of Art through a
Metaphysical Barrier

also goes on two legs, and lacks hooves. This species is greedy, and filthy, and vicious, and cannot be taught to speak; so as the Greeks listened to the speech of aliens, and heard only what sounded like *bar bar bar,* and called them barbarians, so the Houyhnhnms listening to the sounds of the filthy creatures on their island seem to have called them after the most prominent sound to be heard, *Yahoo.* And as the Turing player must decide whether a man can be told from a machine, so the talking horses must decide whether Gulliver can be distinguished from a Yahoo.

Like a computer, he seems strangely tidy; they can observe no organs of generation, nor of excretion, since they do not understand that they are not looking at his hide but at his clothes. And like a machine, he does not eat what the animals do; Yahoo food he shuns, as a Univac would shun hamburgers. So they listen to him speak; and the first thing they must do is teach him their language, which he has little difficulty in learning. This suggests that he is less like a Yahoo than he is like themselves, since the Yahoos cannot be taught anything of this kind.

And now, very strangely, the positions in the Turing Game are shifting; for Gulliver has had to learn the horses' language, which is a grave disadvantage. The Houyhnhnms naturally do not see it as a disadvantage, but we can. For he must use a speech devised by rational animals, exactly as someone who wants to talk to a computer must use Fortran or some other computer language, and avoid entangling the rules of Fortran with attempts at metaphor, hyperbole, synecdoche, or hypothetical expressions. The language Swift devised for the Houyhnhnms is, like the various Universal Languages projected in his time, an early form of Fortran; and its first peculiarity is that all expressions have their face value (what would be the point of wanting to deceive a computer?). All expressions are of two sorts: they either say the thing that is, or the thing that is not; and there is no more purpose in saying the thing that is not, than there is in supplying a machine whose time is costing you five hundred dollars per hour with inaccurate data.

We can see that there is no way for this language to accommodate hypothetical expressions, since to "suppose" that so-and-so is true is to entertain the usefulness of saying the thing that is not; nor can it entertain metaphors, since my love is not a red red rose unless I have made a serious mistake; nor can it manage qualifiers, since either the bare assertion is accurate, needing no adjustments, or inaccurate, and open to reconsideration. You cannot commence the Apostles' Creed in such a language, since it can have no meaning for "believe," and no term for the God whom no one has seen; and as for believing *in* God, what sense can be attached to that? You might believe God, but that is a tautology; of course you believe Him, if He says anything, because when no one says the thing that is not you believe whatever is said.

Under this handicap, then, Gulliver sets out to explain what it is to be human; under a double handicap, what is more, since his mental habits are those of an empiricist, who pretends not to be human anyway. That is no doubt why he learns the Houyhnhnms' language so well. And handicapped alike by the intractable language and his own incomprehension (which we can gauge by the fact that he never once complains about the intractability of the language) he sets out to expound human affairs: a chronicle of uncomprehended externals. So he explains, for instance, the religious conflicts of Europe as vicious disputes over whether the juice of a certain berry be blood or wine, or whether it be better to kiss a post, or to throw it into the fire. (Swift is playing a double game here, as so often, but let it pass.) The more he talks the more confused he grows, and the more ashamed; the more convinced, indeed, that he is at bottom no more than the creature he seems to resemble, a Yahoo. By the time he has decided that the Yahoos are his brethren he has learned the perfect code of Yahoo behavior; so that when he finally sails away from Houyhnhnmland, Swift in a flight of imagination worthy of the proprietors of Buchenwald has him make the sails of his boat out of Yahoo skin: young and fresh Yahoo, because the old ones' skins are too tough.

And all this time his hosts have been imposing on him a set of values proper to rational animals. They have four cardinal virtues, Temperance, Industry, Exercise and Cleanliness, a code accessible alike to the reader of *Playboy* and to Professor B. F. Skinner. The traditional human virtues would be meaningless among rational animals for whom the thing that is not can have no saying, and for whom adaptation to the beneficences of Nature is ultimate truth. For Fortitude implies privations to be met, and Justice implies the workings of the unjust, and Prudence the bitter need to choose between conflicting goods, and Wisdom the insufficiency of either information or shrewdness.

The Houyhnhnms, moreover, educate their young in

strength, speed, and hardiness; there is no need to educate them in anything else, since all else comes naturally. They educate them with judicious impartiality, since the bond between parents and offspring is purely biological, and the obligation purely rational. They regulate births with care, on eugenic principles, matching the strength of one parent with the comeliness of the other. They thread needles, these horses, and they milk cows: what a feat of Swift's, to make us believe *that!* And they have no imaginative literature as we understand it; their poetry makes exact comparisons (because one says the thing that is, and hence takes one's satisfaction in tautologies), and it praises Friendship, Benevolence, and athletic prowess: the oddest derivation from Pindar ever conceived: fancy Diagoras of Rhodes yawning through an encomium in Houyhnhnmese. Had some Homer appeared among them, they would have banished him as a pernicious fabulist. For it is clear how Swift made them up. He borrowed their bodily form from that of the centaur, purified it toward equinity by removing that awkward human thorax, and set them down in what is unmistakably Plato's *Republic*. And Gulliver, though he has read the best books ancient and modern, recognizes none of this.

For virtue, said Socrates, is knowledge, and can be taught; and knowledge is what you know already, if you draw it out of yourself systematically, as the geometrical proof was drawn out of the boy in *Meno*. That is the computer's virtue: knowledge. It has no other virtue except method. It is the perfect rational animal. We build it, then we program it, and what we teach it can be said to be potentially known, so perfectly adapted are those propositions to its inward structure. We keep it Clean, and applaud its Industry and Exercise, and never think to notice its Temperance, so free is it from impulses incompatible with its own well-being. The computer, the third partner in Turing's Game, is the newest incarnation of an old dream, the dream of Socrates who fancied that reason and method delineated the contours of an ideal world, if only poets with their lewd imaginings and unmeasured statements could be prevented from muddling things up. The penchant for composing poetry is a Platonic manifestation of original sin, traceable in equal parts to the laziness which generates muddled statements, and the desire to soothe oneself with postulations of the thing which is not.

And Gulliver resolves to spend the rest of his life, back home among the English Yahoos, modelling his impulses yet more perfectly on those of the noble Houyhnhnms. This last Odysseus, at the end of his journeyings, frequents the stables only of his Ithaca, and talking for hours on end with a pair of horses, does his poor best to fulfill yet another ancient scripture, one of which doubtless he has never heard: the mysterious tradition preserved by the Pyrrhonist chronicler Sextus Empiricus, that Odysseus at the end of his life was metamorphosed into a horse.[24]

And the oddest thing about this odd book is the effect it has had on generations of readers, who have looked up with dismay from the fourth part and concluded, not that Gulliver was mad, but that his author was. The Yahoos, they decide, must be meant for human beings; but what dreadful beings! The Yahoos are themselves, are ourselves, they decide, but how dreadful of Swift to say so! Playing

24. The Loeb Classical Library *Sextus Empiricus*, vol. iv, 149.

yet one more hand of Turing's Game, reader after reader has examined Yahoo, and examined man, and decided that they are identical; and examined Gulliver, and examined man, and decided that they are also identical. The reader is deceived by two counterfeits. The Yahoo is not human at all; Gulliver is not human enough. Gulliver, for whom the Fortran of the horses is the last word in explicit rationality, even becomes a two-legged reasoning horse before our very eyes, without our thinking to protest that something is badly amiss; and we permit ourselves without protest to ascribe to a man who must have been mad, even though he was a clergyman of the Established Church of Ireland, what is by its own premises the only extensive work of English literature written by a horse.

V

Countermeasures

Babbage wrote *Passages from the Life of a Philosopher* in a house in Dorset Street facing Manchester Street, a mere two minutes' walk from Sherlock Holmes' stairway, though that most eminent of counterfeits was not yet in residence. A mile due east, in the reading room of the British Museum, a copy of *The Economy of Manufactures and Machinery* was yielding up footnotes for *Das Kapital* to Karl Marx, the counter-Babbage.

Holmesian, Marxian, Babbagian at once, the modern state was invented in the Victorian factory, the cruelties of which it supposed itself to be remedying. Its people stand idly round at the murders and the gory collisions that punctuate, like occasional blown fuses, the orderly hum of cities; for violence approximates an art form, and as the Greeks had their ritual tragedies and the Elizabethans their bear-baitings, so urban man relishes "happenings," staged or fortuitous.

One spring evening in 1965 perhaps fifty people were treated to a frantic ballet of hate on a Piccadilly sidewalk, thirty yards from the Circus. Four toughs poured as if by prearrangement from a Volkswagen, six from a Citroen, doubleparked for the event. The event: rapid patter of shoeleather on pavement, flailing arms, clinches, break-aways, pointed-shoe kicks to groin, a shopwindow flexing as bodies carom off it, a neckless whiskey bottle rolling on the sidewalk. The spectators drew back twenty-five feet on each side. The battle ended like a sudden shower, then suddenly resumed out of parleyings at car doors. The second round ended; the combatants piled into Volks-wagen and Citroen and drove off grimacing in triumph, shirts ripped, cheeks bloodied, no one maimed: the whole as if choreographed. Then the spectators reformed their cinema queue, awaiting their turn to sit before Clouzot's depiction of huge imperilled trucks loaded with nitro-glycerin, moved over impossible roads against time by men whose fate, as intruders into the filmic universe, was to be mechanized or destroyed or both. Two miles west-ward, in the Kensington Science Museum, four fragments of Babbage engines attest under glass, like Pharaonic mummies, the walking of their souls elsewhere. In Tra-falgar Square it is forbidden to sing without a permit ob-tained from the Ministry of Works.

Such a world, thin, vivid, intermittently turbulent, seems unreal in retrospect and trance-like at the time of immersion. It is the world of any large city, structured by regulations and tacit conventions of noninvolvement, and so far a simulated environment that it resembles Vau-canson's silk-mill, in which temperature and humidity were regulated for the benefit of the silk. And it is a world familiar to readers of post-symbolist poetry; the young Eliot made cities seem like vivid enervating dreams, and Baudelaire experienced them as swarming places where

144

Mr. Charles Babbage, in the Beatific Workshops, Expounds to Mr. Joseph F. Keaton, Recently Arrived, the Workings of the Analytical Engine

spectres accost you at noon. The post-symbolist aesthetic —its suave surfaces, its unnerving discontinuities—remains to this day consistent with what is there to be felt in London or Los Angeles. Poemscape and cityscape are highly organized modes of non-reality, mutually elucidative. Both are simulated environments for the mind, arrived at by taking thought, and as if anonymously. If we want to discover why so much reality seems to have been withdrawn from the urban experience, so that systems admonish as bloodlessly as Houyhnhnms, the arts can enlighten us, precisely as they enlighten us about the nature of counterfeiting; and when we find the arts in turn taking that unreality for their subject, and producing their effects much as it is produced, we shall be ready to comprehend the truth that artists counterfeit in a counterfeiting time, to save us from debility amid the conventions of empiricism in a milieu where we are placed, empiric observers, before much that custom forbids us to quite understand.

These arts resemble, indeed simulate, phenomena from which the careless do not distinguish them: mere expressions of the time, written, drawn, fabricated, enacted, which are part of the counterfeit milieu itself, and which suggest, for instance, that chaotic outbursts give hope, as protests against drabness.

The queuers knew better, having had enough experience of the urban continuum to accept such convections (formal as mushroom clouds) without panic. And two centuries' carefully-plotted fiction has surely instructed us that wherever anarchy may get its energy, it draws its forms and occasions directly from the order in which the anarchists move and by which they are shaped. From *Moll*

Flanders (1722) to *Bleak House* (1852) and *Lucky Jim* (1954), novel after novel has demonstrated how rogues (intelligible, like all fictional characters, because automated) are qualified denizens of an intelligible because automated world. Both pursue intelligible goals, and the same ones, and by the same means, and the Dickens who hated the blacking-factory pridefully enslaved himself in a novel-factory. ("Mr. Babbage will presently invent a Novel-writing machine," wrote Emerson in his journal for August 2, 1842; and did not Poe forecast the resolution of *Barnaby Rudge,* quite as if he had divined the Novel-Engine's program?)

For the connection between the humdrum and the catastrophic should not surprise us, when the grotesque is the natural flowering of the orderly. The grotesque man, the man of sense, thinks himself quintessentially orderly, as the stuffed-owl poet thinks his assertions poetical. And as metaphysics contains physics, including its difficulties, and metamathematics contains daily mathematics, including such awkward consequences of daily mathematics as the set of all infinite sets, so we have seen Keaton and Pope creating in different arts, two centuries apart, a metagrotesquerie to accommodate in its higher order of agility the situations, acrobatic or verbal, in which men land by being perfectly reasonable. This meant, for both men, counterfeiting the actions of beings less agile than they. Pope, never deviating from his resolve to be England's first "correct" poet, worked toward this ambition partly by shamming cacophonous incompetence. Keaton, playing a character very largely himself who was nonetheless all thumbs and only saved (when saved) by miraculous interventions into a cosmos he was unequipped to cope with, himself contrived both the miracles and the contrivances from which they delivered him. For Babbage, one consequence of the working of the Difference Engine was that it proved the possibility of miracles,[1] as for Turing the point of conceiving the Turing Machine was to prove that certain propositions were undecidable, and that a closed system could therefore contain surprises.[2] In 1931 Kurt Gödel was able to show that the *Principia Mathematica* was capable of proving neither its own consistency nor *all* of its constituent propositions: carefully though the *Principia* had been put together, out of interdependent, accurately-fitted parts.[3] A system of logic, a perfectly logical machine, is so far from wholly predictable that it cannot, Turing showed, even predict what it can or cannot do, and this when it is functioning perfectly. This truth, which the great comedians seem to have known intuitively, belies the Romantic notion that machines are models of tragic implacability, and it is not surprising to learn that Keaton for one was a considerable mechanician. He devised among other things a Venetian Blind Opener, which after "a long mechanical churning" delivered "a one-minute explosion

1. Charles Babbage, *Ninth Bridgewater Treatise*, London, 1837. In another part of this book he postulated the chance of a man rising from the dead as 1 in 10^{12}.
2. Turing, "On Computable Numbers . . ." *Proc. Lond. Math. Soc.*, ser. 2, vol. 42, 230-265 [1937]. Turing showed that there is no method of showing whether a given formula within a system is provable, unless by proving it. There is also no way of getting a machine to tell you whether it can write *Hamlet* unless you supply the entire text of *Hamlet* by way of making the question specific, but that is another story.
3. For a detailed exposition see Ernest Nagel and James R. Newman, "Goedel's Proof," in *Newman, The World of Mathematics*, N. Y., 1956, vol. III, 1668-1695. An English version of Gödel's paper is given in M. Davis, *The Undecidable*, 5-38.

of events: the venetian blinds flew up, a .32-caliber pistol shot off a blank cartridge, and while an Edison phonograph played John Philip Sousa's 'Hail to the Chief,' up from behind the sofa, on wires, shot a large picture of Louis B. Mayer."[4] It interested *Popular Mechanics* and the engineers from Consolidated Aircraft, and might have starred in any exhibition of kinetic sculpture had it not seemed to subvert not only pushbutton man and Mr. Mayer but, in its really triumphant uselessness, kinetic sculpture itself. For mechanism yearns to parody itself, and so does any man imbued with its logic. Dickens' vision was impaired by ideology when he created Gradgrind, and Agatha Christie's sounder when she perceived in Hercule Poirot (of the "little gray cells") a touch of absurdity. Consider Babbage once more.

Babbage inhabits both the rational world and the world of the factory, and by his rigor as by his enthusiasm for process demonstrates their thorough compatibility. And into what bizarre postures does rationality not force him! Not even when hot in pursuit of organ grinders does his behavior manifest a trace of Gradgrind's rigidity. One very cold day, while conducting experiments on the momentum of railway cars, he found himself on a detached wagon far from the terminus; but wrapped around his person was a length of cloth, three yards in fact, coarse and blue, which he had purchased to protect himself from the wind. "This I now unwound; we held it up as a sail, and gradually acquiring greater velocity, finally reached and sailed across the whole of the Hanwell viaduct at a very fair pace."[5] This is quintessentially Keatonian. So is

4. Rudi Blesh, *Keaton*, 350.
5. Babbage, *Passages from the Life of a Philosopher*, 325-6.

the stomach pump he took round the courts of Europe for a conversation piece, as travelers to Africa used to take beads. So are his antics at the head of a mob of street musicians and loiterers, as he marches in quest of a bobby. So was his day in the crater of Vesuvius, a dark plain veined with fiery cracks, to attain which he slid and stumbled down the rubble, with "one of Troughton's heavy barometers" strapped to his back, "an excellent box sextant" in his pocket, and "in a rough kind of basket two or three thermometers, a measuring tape, and a glass bottle enclosed in a leather case, commonly called a pocket-pistol, accompanied by a few biscuits." The bottle held Irish whiskey. To determine the height of the rim from which he had descended, he measured off a 340-foot base line on the scoriac soil, marking one end with his walking stick. The walking stick burst into flames. Then addressing his attention to the active crater, he timed its eructations and after some maneuvering installed himself at full length, with six minutes to spare before the next burst, on a ledge of rock overhanging the lake of lava. He was "armed with two phials, one of common smelling salts, and the other containing a solution of ammonia," the former to counteract dizziness, the latter acid vapors: method, in case of crisis, being applicable both to observer and to observed. He examined minutely the propagation of waves in fluid rock, returned to safety when his watch bade, and consumed biscuits. Romanticism's long romance with volcanism having yielded at last to smelling salts and the chronometer, he descended to Naples, a satisfying day behind him. His boots disintegrated when he tried to remove them.[6]

6. Babbage, *Passages*, 216-222.

This rational world of his is the one simulated by the Engine, that number-factory. The Engine, a Turing Machine in brass (Turing himself said so), is like the Turing Machine a virtuoso of simulation, thus a player of the Turing Game, thus a potential imitator of man. Being a rational animal (the brass wheels give it animality) it is an imitator of man, as is a Houyhnhnm. And conceived as it is in the image of its creator, the Analytical Engine suggests that Babbage himself, the Ur-Keaton, the post-Gulliverian man, the "mathematical Timon" who hated, said a contemporary, "mankind in general, Englishmen in particular, and the English government and organ-grinders most of all"[7]: Babbage is somehow himself an imitation man, the counterfeit of some elusive *humanitas*.

He is gay, as Yeats said Hamlet and Lear were gay. Yet the flaming staff and crumbling boots are indices of the danger. Method, order, the division of labor, these mask from him all but the methodizable implications of what he is about. The volcano is an occasion for instruments, notes and biscuits: so much for Byron. Uncommissioned music is a cue to summon police: so much for Blake. Satire is a check list of the possible: so much for Swift: for he explicitly points out wherein technology has outstripped Lagado: "light almost solar has been extracted from the refuse of fish; fire has been sifted by the lamp of Davy; and machinery has been taught arithmetic instead of poetry."[8] And as to the lordly Houyhnhnm, the lordly Houyhnhnm, or rather, dead horse, may still (1846), due. method aiding, minister to our enlightenment, illustrating

7. Morrison and Morrison, *Babbage*, xiii.
8. Babbage, *Economy of Manufactures*, sec. 344.

as he does "the profitable conversion of substances apparently of no value." For "the hair is first cut off from the mane and tail. It amounts usually to about a quarter of a pound, which, at 5*d* per lb. is worth 1¼ *d*." Next the skin; next the blood (for refining sugar, for manure, exported to America, and for fattening "pigeons, poultry, and especially turkeys," though these to be sure once fattened should be fed with grain a few days before they are killed, to restore the flavor); next the shoes (old iron) and the hoofs (combs, sal ammonia, Prussian blue). The fat will make soap or gas, or grease live Houyhnhnms' harness, and also give off in combustion a standard of heat "demanded by enamellers and glass toy makers." A well-fed horse will yield sixty pounds of this commodity, but a nag about eight. The flesh feeds workmen, cats, dogs, pigs, and even poultry. The tendons make glue, the bones fans, the small intestines coarse strings for lathes. All this dismemberment breeds maggots, which bait fishhooks and feed pheasants; and draws (through special holes around the workshop) rats—unsung by any Muse, four-thousand per week— whose skins the furriers purchase "at about 3*s*. the hundred." Ratskins, maggots, intestines, bones, tendons, flesh, fat, hooves, shoes, blood, skin, hair: though humiliated by his Platonic essence, Horsepower, (which by definition is some fifty percent in excess of the average power of the average horse) the Houyhnhnm conquers, divided, Economic Death. Gulliver's mentors would have been the first to applaud their own dismemberment, the apotheosis of their own view of their own lives. Let Engines, rated in Horsepower, counterfeit his Strength, Speed, and Hardiness; he is secure as brass and steam are not in the possession of blood, bones, hoofs and fat and intestines, the sale of which will maintain the men who maintain his offspring ("They will have it that *Nature* teaches them to love the whole Species," wrote Swift, all whose love was "toward individuals."[9]) Horse sense has passed into the Analytical Engine; having which, what need have Gulliver's descendants of Houyhnhnms, except to oil its wheels and grease its belts? Now the carcass that fetched merely 8*s*. 6*d*. at the knacker's door puts on immortality in the lathes and gluepots of the new Laputa, where they tabulate lore of this kind:

		£	*s.*	*d.*
1.	Hair	0	0	1¼
2.	Skin	0	9	0
3.	Blood	0	1	9
4.	Shoes and nails	0	0	2½
5.	Hoofs	0	1	5
6.	Fat	0	4	0
7.	Flesh	1	8	0
8.	Tendons	0	0	3
9.	Bones	0	2	0
10.	Intestines			
11.	Maggots	0	1	5
12.	Rats			
		£2.	8.	1¾

The hairs of his tail are numbered; he is of more value than many sparrows; by his tripes (the glue-pot intervening) we are sealed.[10] In urban North America today barely a horse remains, though paperback Gullivers proliferate to serve the curricula and motor manufacturers

9. See his letter to Alexander Pope, Sept. 29, 1725.
10. This extraordinary analysis is given in an appendix added to the *Economy of Manufactures* in 1846.

engage in horsepower races. (Three hundred horsepower! Imagine three hundred horses!)

In the midst of Babbage's triumphant demonstration the horse has somehow disappeared; so much so that we can derive no idea of what Swift fully meant us to receive from *Gulliver IV*, because we have no experience of a society substantially dependent on horses. They were not only the animals logic texts contrasted with man, duly equipped with the property of whinnying (*facultas hinniendi*), and slyly transposed by Swift from the irrational to the rational side of the page;[11] not only allegories of the horsey English, set over Yahoos who resemble the Hibernian peasants; not only grotesque visions, milking their cows: they were, muscular, graceful, ubiquitous, everywhere one turned all men's auxiliaries, the pervasive mode of transport, the sinews of trade and commerce, beasts from whose dung steam rose every nippy morning, imagined by the satirist as taking civilization over. (Promiscuous excrement denotes horses in a city, but Yahoos in Swift.) Just so Keaton, whose Fords more than once spread flat their wheels and lay down under him, imagined the car taking over, and the city under its latent aspect of menace transformed into one huge malevolent flux of Traffic, which only the Cop could mediate. But Keaton's Cop too has faded, like the horse; the cop of the silent screen is absurd to us; to Keaton's screen self he was Gestapo-like. So with the Keaton car; modern eyes see, in those films, absurd spindly imitation cars that could be flown like box-kites in a moderate gale. Satire, the art

11. See R. S. Crane, "The Houyhnhnms, the Yahoos, and the History of Ideas," in J. A. Mazzeo, ed. *Reason and Imagination*, N. Y., 1962, 248.

form of objective truth, gives up its gristly immediacy as externals mutate, and shows posterity schematic ghosts.

Keaton's contemporary, Chaplin, it is an effort to recall, grimaced in a world where bowels move and dead dogs smell. James Agee remembered how it seemed at the time to a boy—"and there was Charlie, flat on his bottom on the sidewalk, and the way he looked, kind of sickly and disgusted, you could see that he suddenly remembered those eggs, and suddenly you remembered them too. The way his face looked, with the lips wrinkled off the teeth and the sickly little smile, it made you feel just the way those broken eggs must feel aginst your seat, as queer and awful as that time in the white pekay suit, when it ran down out of the pants-legs and showed all over your stockings and you had to walk home that way with people looking; and Rufus' father nearly tore his head off laughing and so did everybody else. . . . And then it was even funnier when Charlie very carefully got himself up from the sidewalk, with that sickly look even worse on his face, and put his cane under one arm, and began to pick at his pants, front and back, very carefully, with his fingers crooked, as if it were too dirty to touch, picking the sticky cloth away from his skin."[12] We remember Chaplin now for a choreographic finesse.

So past satire grows disembodied. An art so readily emptied of its particulars, so readily reducible to intelligible form, so pure and apparently complete when so reduced, is at center an art of ideas. That is why *Gulliver's Travels,* with the omission of a few cloacal passages, will

12. James Agee, *A Death in the Family,* N. Y., 1957, ch. I.

turn into a children's book. Juvenal's satire is difficult to draw into the same discussion with Swift's precisely for this reason, that Juvenal accretes irreducibly noxious particulars—crowded houses propped up as by straws, slops emptied onto one's head; we respond to these or to nothing. But eighteenth century satire traffics in epistemologies, which the particulars merely render apprehensible. *The Dunciad* too, once so tinglingly topical, has as Pope foresaw survived anyone's interest in any of the Dunces, and reads now like a Schoenberg composition astonishingly generated by a contemporary of Handel's. This is a persistent theme of modern times, this tendency of topical arts to become formal. Cities, we have seen, do the same.

And to see art in this way progressively losing its skin and bowels, progressively firming and flexing its epistemological skeleton, is to see mimed the retreat of all experience whatever from full apprehensibility (hence the shrill rage of Lawrence). It is always so, in the realm of the counterfeiters. Imagination, grown specialized, is not fed on visions but is curious about applications. A sculpture by Len Lye or Jean Tingueley, a black-on-black by Ad Reinhardt, is less a manual achievement than an idea, which having seen we could almost reproduce at home. And we need not think of reproducing Andy Warhol's tins, boxes and movies, we need not even see them; he has devised an art of pure idea, whose very material is Publicity, as Michelangelo's was stone.

The nature of events, like that of artifacts, is obscured by their power to illustrate some idea. Charles Babbage describes an accident which occurred to a whaleboat:

> The line of the harpoon being fastened to it, the whale in this instance dived directly down, and carried the boat along with him. On returning to the surface the animal was killed, but the boat, instead of rising, was found suspended beneath the whale by the rope of the harpoon; and on drawing it up, every part of the wood was found to be so completely saturated with water as to sink immediately to the bottom.[13]

We can guess how John Donne's mind would have embodied such a tale: into what intuitions of a ruined cosmos he would have assimilated that leaden boat hung in the deep from beneath Leviathan, as he assimilated the work of globe-makers to sorrow's knack for omnipresence. But Babbage tells it not as a minatory or awesome tale but as a fact: a fact "stated by Mr. Scoresby" and having this value, that it gives an idea of "the quantity of matter which can be injected into wood, by great pressure," so suggesting the feasibility of impregnating wood with a rot-resistant or fire-resistant chemical. The men in the whaleboat, if the whale's dive killed them, may be assured, in that higher world where the Analytical Engine no doubt stands gleaming and completed, that they once participated in a physical demonstration, recorded for men's enlightenment in the *Economy of Manufactures.*

For the satirist, for the technician, and for the counterfeiter, fact tends to behave in this way: retaining its contours, altering its nature. The creative imagination in our time has gone deep into this principle, and exploits it

13. Babbage, *Economy*, sec. 34.

habitually. Consider an anecdote from the German occupation of France:

Two men have been sent into the country to make a rendezvous with a third, whom they have never seen and know only by a code name. They work hard at making their presence and movements seem natural, an especial challenge since they seem to have no cover story. They scrounge vegetables, sleep in ditches, submit like tramps to indignities and beatings: and at the appointed spot no one meets them. Should they move on or stay? It seems best to stay; the normal prudence of the underground has withheld from them any clue to the significance of their rendezvous, but they cannot assume that its significance is slight. So they set about the business of waiting, on a country road, at evening, not too obtrusively. The tax on their resources is enormous. A refugee passes, his servant loaded with belongings; they are so relieved to see anyone at all that they almost give their mission away. Then a boy runs up with a message: "Mr. Godot told me to tell you he won't come this evening but surely tomorrow:" and they are committed to a second time of waiting, more deadly than the first.

It seems reasonable to guess that Beckett's play had some such germ[14]: but if so Beckett has already done to the play what time did to the Houyhnhnms: he has withdrawn the anecdotal specificities and left a distilled waiting to accrete what meanings it can. A few traces of the war years remain: the encumbered journeying of Pozzo and Lucky, the apathy with which mysterious blind-

14. It should be emphasized that this account of the play's origin is pure speculation. Beckett was in France during the occupation, and was involved with the Resistance.

ings are accepted, the two friends' panic when they suppose themselves surrounded, the land's ravaged look and the bitter promise implied by a few leaves, the importance of conferring on inaction a style that will draw no attention from the dispensers of beatings—

—I tell you I wasn't doing anything.
—Perhaps you weren't. But it's the way of doing it
   that counts, the way of doing it, if you want to
   go on living . . .

the tacit premise that one does not explain the company one is in, and moment by moment a meaninglessness which we gather was not always there, but in these seemingly unending times is pervasive.

These details, of course, cohere with the tone of the play, with its ambient mysteriousness. The reader is not tempted to look around for a time and place to which they will attach. But a few references to Germans and sector chiefs would have told us to say that the play is "about the Occupation." As things are, it is difficult to say what it is about, except about waiting, and so powerful is the experience of a play about waiting, once we have experienced it, that no adduction of Occupation detail will distract us. We have meaning, then, without specific content, and we have this disconcerting effect thanks to the counterfeiter's central strategy, which is to suppress traces of origin. That one does not know what modern works are "about" is a frequent complaint, and a misguided complaint since it is their most deliberated characteristic. (And where do book matches come from? Circulars? Old keys? It is a more familiar universe than it seems.)

To fake, as it were, an antique; to let a work issue from the workshop already marked as time marks human artifacts: this is the methodology behind many of our time's masterworks. There is nothing in *Waiting for Godot* to become "period," because the period allusions were never put in, not even in 1947 when they would have seemed indistinguishable from the domain of common nouns. A similar play, come down from, say, the time of Dostoyevsky, would have stirred revolutionary emotions then but would seem an image of brute endurance now. There seems wisdom in aiming directly at what one can judge will be the ultimate effect. Yeats wrote plays implying that a Celtic mythology was as familiar to his audience as the genealogies of Atreus were to the Greeks; they seemed strange and very old plays the day they were first performed, and decades have not made them seem a day older. A painting long called *The Night Watch* was made in collaboration by Rembrandt, who did a brilliant rendition of Captain Cocq's company of the Civil Guard, and Time, which darkened his varnish till only glints and highlights penetrated what seemed nocturnal murk. When three centuries later restorers brought back Captain Cocq's gay company, there were cries of outrage at the vanishing of the Night Watch, as though Time had been the more deeply inspired member of the partnership. Yet further time might have made the great canvas virtually black-on-black, and Reinhardt's black-on-blacks are not only challenges to our vision, but perhaps comments on the process that lends patina: whoever loves an almost invisible oil four hundred years old should love these directly. Wordsworth exists as the author of perhaps two hundred pages; so does Eliot; but the two hundred pages were selected in Wordsworth's case by Time (with a succession of assistants) and in Eliot's case by Eliot, before publication. To call the 1925 volume which ran from "Prufrock" to "The Hollow Men" his *Poems* was nearly as humorous a gesture as that of Max Beerbohm, when at twenty-three he issued in a little book his *Works*. A poem by Sappho, after two millenia's ravishing of the parchment, looks like this:

```
[              ] of Eros, anxious [           ]
[                                             ]
[         ] I admire, I gaze at you [        ]
[         ] Ermiona herself, and like her
[              ] you are as blonde as Elena,
[Decorous, suave].
[                    ] to mortal women, but know this
[      ] me [         ] all solicitude
[                              ] but
[               ] dew of the riverside, gleaming
[                                             ]
[         ] to make it last all night long.
```

A passage of Ezra Pound's, exactly as it went to the printer in 1959, looks like this:

```
Yao and Shun ruled by jade
        That the goddess turn crystal within her
This is grain rite
        Luigi on the hill path
                        this is grain rite
near Enna, at Nyssa:
                Circe, Persephone
so different is sea from glen that
                the juniper is her holy bush
between the two pine trees, not Circe
        but Circe was like that
                coming from the house of smooth stone
'not know which god'
                nor could enter her eyes by probing
        the light blazed behind her
                nor was this from sunset.[15]
```

15. Sappho, *Poems and Fragments*, tr. Guy Davenport, Ann Arbor, 1965, No. 42 [Lobel & Page 23]; and Ezra Pound, Canto 106 (*Thrones*, p. 106).

Time's ellipses work at random, Pound's do not; but Pound's ellipses are like attempts to simulate what a decay as beneficent as the one that produced *The Night Watch* might do to an archaic poem.

So just as satire, the by-product of counterfeiting, is lightened of its documentary weight by time, imagination counterfeiting the work of time seeks to pare things away in advance, and the classics of our age resemble in more than one way simulated Classics.

The classics of our age are equally concerned with another theme developed by counterfeiting, the nice discrimination between realities and their simulacra. Thus Eliot's Simeon, whose voice has the enervation of death, is a saint, and Eliot's Gerontion, whose enjambments mime the pressure of valiant breath, is deep down in a funnel of wind. "Gerontion," correspondingly, which resembles a fragment of a Jacobean play, implies no plot and agitates a formal void, while "A Song for Simeon," which resembles the production of utter fatigue, locks tightly into a scriptural context and has rhymes for all but six of its thirty-seven lines. They are careful counter-poems, exchanging images. Eliot's Hollow Men, yearning toward.

> The hope only
> Of empty men,

though themselves empty men for whom that hope is only a hope, resemble to the untrained eye those valiant men who have emptied themselves, and for whom only it can be a hope; for "The soul cannot be possessed by the divine union, until it has divested itself of the love of created beings." To train the untrained eye which cannot tell hollow men from men self-divested is the business of *Murder in the Cathedral,* in which the Knights try to represent as suicide what the audience has understood to be self-surrender, and in which Thomas himself is made to confront the knife-edge between seeking death and resigning himself to it. From the outside one cannot tell, as from the outside it would be impossible to say that an ideal Vaucanson duck had or had not emerged from an egg; for the suicide is an exact counterfeit of the martyr, and Eliot's theme is precisely that the histories that memorialize Thomas à Becket do not care. All Eliot's enervated men are simulated saints, and the sanctity his late work seeks to define made many readers suppose that a spent poet was contriving simulacra of his early inspiration.[16]

Two prophetic novels by Wyndham Lewis (1882-1957) succeed, while manipulating a grittily realistic texture, in offering for our inspection a whole world feeding on the counterfeit. In *The Revenge for Love* (1937) an honest second-rate artist is briefly employed by a Van Gogh factory ("You wouldn't have to forge *the signatures!* Only *the pictures!*"). Its proprietors have arrived at the political insight that all rewards are reserved for simulations.

> He had formulas, by this time, for everything. The pupils of the eyes, for instance, in a typical Van Gogh, were painted—it was Tristy had pointed this out—as a nest of concentric wedges of greens, reds, blues and yellows, with their apex inwards. He had got the trick of that. And he had mastered the bald look of the pale eyebrows, which marked the base of the bony swellings. Then more wedges stuck on end, a miniature hedge of them, for the

16. See my *The Invisible Poet: T. S. Eliot,* N. Y., 1959, for a detailed exposition.

tissue of the lips. He could do a Van Gogh self-
mouth pretty well by this time.[17]

When he rebels, his masters, a phony artist and a phony
Maecenas, con him into running a truckload of arms into
Spain for the benefit of the pseudo-Workers. But the
truck's false bottom secretes only bricks; his is a decoy
mission, certified to by a letter bearing a forgery of his
own signature, and he falls over a cliff to his death, the
bottom, according to the metaphor that pervades the
book, having dropped out of this ramshackle universe.

In *The Vulgar Streak* (1941) a man who has remade
himself from scratch, eradicating every trace of working
class speech and acquiring the accent and manners that
will equip him to get on in the circles where money flows,
turns out to be by profession a passer of counterfeit money,
and when he is cornered hangs himself. Lewis is careful
to make the point that actual money, with its reference to
nonexistent gold, is neither physically nor metaphysically
distinguishable from the basement product, nor are actual
manners, accents, skills. They are merely authorized,
whereas home-brew is unauthorized. The counterfeit, as
we clearly understand by now, does not claim a reality it
does not possess, but only an origin—that is, an authori-
zation.

You forge a signature, Lewis informs us in *The Revenge
for Love,* not by modifying your own handwriting to make
it resemble another's, but by abandoning handwriting; you
turn the model upside down and draw what you see. You
do not become, however slightly, someone else, assimi-
lating his tidiness or his bravura: you become the manual

17. Wyndham Lewis, *The Revenge for Love,* VI.2.

executant merely of something that is meaningless until inverted. In short you become nobody, as the empiricist always makes himself into nobody. Lewis learned this trick, it is amusing to know, from the celebrated amateur forger and music box collector A. J. A. Symons, a man who, like the protagonist of every Lewis novel, enjoyed the challenge of so deliberately shaping his own personality that people would intuit on his behalf a past and a social status that had never existed. His short life (1900-1941) was, notably on its financial side, an intricate and largely harmless confidence game, and the subject of his principal work, *The Quest for Corvo,* was a man born Frederick Rolfe who claimed a nonexistent baronetcy, lived by his wits, endeavored to counter public disesteem of the Borgia, and like his biographer flaunted an elaborately contrived handwriting. The first sentence details the circumstances of Symons' own interest in Corvo; Symons' own biographer in turn tells us it is untrue.[18] Corvo in turn . . . but we need not pursue down labyrinths of dandyism an infinite regress. Suffice it to notice that whatever Symons may have contributed to the central character in *The Vulgar Streak* we owe to Lewis's zestful connoisseurship of the spurious.

The dandy takes his whole life as material for a walking work of art, and the pathology of dandyism, shorn of its romance, was Lewis's lifelong subject. Perceiving his subject everywhere—it had been permeating English society since the eighteenth century, to the point where it was nearly impossible to tell an aristocrat from an automaton —he expended appalling energies finding counterfeit uni-

18. See J. Symons, *A. J. A. Symons, his Life and Speculations,* London, 1950, and W. K. Rose, ed., *The Letters of Wyndham Lewis,* N. Y., 1963.

verses outrageous, and nearly equal energies inventing them. For there is great freedom in a cosmos accessible to the imprint of your will, and yet some evident hitch in a frame of things that throws you back on your own will so completely. Lewis would have preferred, in many moods, a closed system, to sustain and guide his abilities. He seems not to have known, except with the dark side of his mind, that as it is the ambition of all explanations to be complete, so all systems will their own closure, and the system that has prevailed since empiricism first dawned is as closed as such things can be. That system has spawned, as its natural derivative, the activity of the counterfeiter, and thanks to his energies has very nearly duplicated itself inside itself. His energies in turn are the relevant imaginative energies to free us from the blandishments of the spurious, for every closed system has a floating center, which genius somehow discovers.

"Spontaneity" does not rebuke the system; spontaneity is the system's conditioned reflex, as the Piccadilly queue understood when the cars discharged ten flailing automata, and some minutes later reabsorbed them. Spontaneity's liaisons with the spurious go so deep that the natural product of such a fake-masterpiece factory as Lewis presents is counterfeit Van Goghs: for spontaneity systematizes itself into mannerisms, bold and readily imitated (". . . a nest of concentric wedges of greens, reds, blues and yellows . . ."). Such artifacts abound: jolly starlets created by press-agentry, "demonstrations" synthesized by crowd-engineers out of handbooks mimeographed by retired revolutionaries. And as Defoe and Swift counterfeited in a counterfeiting time, so in these times of synthetic freedom the creative imagination does what the times do; from the very beginning of the *vers-libre* movement fifty years ago the art of master after master has assumed the risk of being mistaken for anarchy. William Carlos Williams carried small poems through draft after draft, retyping them with minute variants of diction and lineation, in quest of the form that would seem to have dropped without forethought out of the typewriter, and would seem furthermore to be merely what someone had *said*:

> She smiled—
> Yes, you do what you please
> first, then I can do what I please

which became

> She smiled—
> Yes, you do what you please first,
> then I can do what I please—

and finally

> She smiled. Yes,
> you do what you please first
> then I can do what I please—

The little poem "At the Bar"—

> Hi, open up a dozen.
>
> Wha'cha tryin' ta do—
> charge ya batteries?
>
> Make it two.
>
> Easy girl!
> You'll blow a fuse if
> ya keep that up.

—went through five typescripts from which we can recover seven different versions of the last speech, for instance

> Take it easy. You'll
> blow a fuse if you keep that up

and

> Easy girl! You'll blow
> a fuse if ya keep
> that up.[19]

It is not news that poets revise; but Williams' effort was to revise out of sight, not the fact that pains had been taken, but the fact that there had even been a poet. Robert Creeley, who has professed admiration for the forms of Coleridge, erases, so to speak, the borders of a sentence, to leave not a formal ellipse but the part the voice emphasizes:

> The love of a woman
> is the possibility which
> surrounds her as hair
> her head, as the love of her
>
> follows and describes
> her. But what if
> they die, then there is
> still the aura
>
> left, left sadly, but
> hovers in the air, surely,
> where this had taken place?
> Then sing, of her, of whom
>
> it will be said, he
> sang of her, it was the
> song he made which made her
> happy, so she lived.[20]

19. William Carlos Williams, *Collected Earlier Poems*, Norfolk, 1951. See "The Last Words of my English Grandmother" (443) and "At the Bar" (431). The draft versions are in the Poetry Room, Lockwood Memorial Library, State University of New York at Buffalo. They are quoted here by the Library's permission and that of Mrs. William Carlos Williams.
20. Robert Creeley, *For Love: poems 1950-1960*, N. Y., 1962, 142.

—which is like a song of Campion's reproduced in water-color. If such crafted impromptus have suggested to some that today's authentic art has leave to be licentious, or to others that not showing traces of the T-square they cannot be authentic art, the suggestible are to blame for their own misconceptions. Spontaneity is both the easiest and the hardest thing in the world to imitate, and art's vocation is always to do the hard way what is being done easily. Such poetry, like the painting of Matisse, mirrors and belies a world of *New Yorker* advertisements and factory-made Van Goghs.

The focus of counterfeiting is always on origins, and behind such poetry there seems to be not only no craft but no poet: as though the language had gathered itself into form, as flames do or clouds. Behind the machine in the Turing Game there seems to be a man's lifetime, though all its traces were programmed in yesterday. Or rather, not yesterday: there is a fallacy we have hitherto skirted. Turing calculated that the 10^7 bits of information required might be generated by sixty programmers working steadily for fifty years, "if nothing went into the waste-paper basket," and proposed instead to imitate nature's way, treating the machine as a child and then educating it. This should be possible, he thought, because the child, in developing the power to generalize and to "learn from experience," accomplishes much of his own education. The child, as he understood it, is a Lockean *tabula rasa*:

> Presumably the child-brain is something like a note-book as one buys it from the stationers. Rather little mechanism, and lots of blank sheets. (Mechanism and writing are from our point of view almost

synonymous.) Our hope is that there is so little mechanism in the child-brain that something like it can be easily programmed. The amount of work in the education we can assume, as a first approximation, to be much the same as for the human child.[21]

This child-machine, like any other adaptation of the Turing Machine, has only this aptitude, that each state follows necessarily from the previous one, so everything is learnt by receiving stimuli, comparing them, and drawing necessary inferences. The rapidity of Turing's sketch of the educational process—a few hundred words at the end of a ten-thousand-word paper—testifies to the degree of his readers' acceptance of such a model. The child who is father of the man has not really changed, for the scientific mind, since Locke. It is permissible to say, as we have said before of Turing, that he may quite legitimately be read as a satirist, describing in careful detail the child who is destined to be the father of Lemuel Gulliver.

But this is a counterfeit child, who will learn to speak about the time Vaucanson's duck learns to lay an egg. As speech, in the Ciceronian tradition, distinguishes man from the brutes, so (said Descartes) does it distinguish man from the automaton, from the simulated man. An immense amount of programming is required to teach a Turing automaton to utter three or four convincing sentences; but with much less effort we can set a child on the way to talking for the rest of his life, and uttering (as Noam Chomsky points out[22]) thousands of sentences he has never heard, all quite grammatical. This is so striking a

21. Turing, "Thought and Machine Intelligence," sec. 7.
22. N. Chomsky, *Cartesian Linguistics*, N. Y., 1966, 65, also note 114.

fact that one would have expected a programmer or two to be arrested by it; on the contrary, immense effort has been devoted to persuading us that a child, with a somewhat weaker endowment than a Turing Machine, learns something as intricate as a language by trial and error. Though we do not understand the rules of sentence construction sufficiently well to explain them to a computer, we are expected to believe that an eight-year-old, who seems to understand them intuitively, has arrived at that understanding in a very short time by trial and error, reward and punishment, stimulus and response and reinforcement.

Much effort, in short, has been devoted to persuading us that we really are rather slipshod automata, which thanks to modern education can be taught a few things, such as Temperance, Industry, Exercise and Cleanliness. We can also be connected to meters and shown television programs, and the meters, by registering variations in our skin's electrical resistance, will tell our masters which programs entertain us best.

A child learning to speak, were some wise men from Brobdingnag to examine him, would resemble a mysterious device that accepts as input "very scattered and inadequate data," and generates as output an amazingly uniform product, exceeding the input in quantity and very often in quality (were Shakespeare's teachers more eloquent than he?). It would be natural for the wise men to suppose that the device in question—we may call it the learning mind—has a structure to account for these surprising disparities, certainly a structure transcending that of a Turing Machine. But many busy folk think not, and have lent their talents to creating an environment (of learning, of politics, of entertainment, of educational theory) perfectly appropriate for a world full of quick little dummies. Teaching Machines, in this world, "reinforce" responses, repeating simple notions over and over, and encouraging compliance with simulated delight. This is a counterfeit world for the counterfeit person. Within it further counterfeiting—known as "Art"—helps maintain human sanity. Wisdom is in part the ability to tell one mode of counterfeit from the other, that which constitutes the aggressive environment from that which is beneficent and homeopathic.

Empiricism is a game. Its central rule forbids you to understand what you are talking about. The application of this rule, when we remember that we *are* playing a game, yields satire. Satire's particulars fade, its structure stays; and from within the structure a ghostly person grimaces, to catch sight of whom, as to see Alan Turing on his bicycle or Jonathan Swift manipulating his language-fields, is to command the vision which makes the whole intelligible. Bits of apparent insanity can keep us oriented: a man faking soup labels, a man writing a play about men doing nothing, a poet writing an incompetent poet's poem, a man forcing grammar and syntax to simulate, as clockwork simulated the movements of a duck, a few words exchanged in a New Jersey bar. These things, once done, seem too to have unaccountably "happened" (who would take trouble over them?), for Art too pretends to withdraw the conceiving person, while reconstituting spontaneities so that they look like "behavior." If you are wise you are not deceived. Assaying for traces of the controlling person whatever offers itself to you as experience, you seek equilibrium in a universe constituted wholly of things synthesized out of facts: magazine articles, nonfictional fictions, doctoral theses, judicial testimony; published nonbooks and reported nonevents; retouched photographs, dubbed recordings, actors, talking dolls; the *Ulysses* of Joyce and the *Cantos* of Pound; Beats (pop Franciscans), psychedelics (pop mysticism); Disneyland, the *Labyrinths* of Borges; interviews, autobiographies, newspapers, surveys; *Gulliver's Travels*, core curricula; Piltdown Man and the Noble Savage; those eminent writers of fiction Charles Dickens and Charles Darwin; those prolific disseminators of artifacts the Campbell's Soup Company and Pablo Picasso; flight simulators, dioramas; and books such as the one you have just finished reading.